THE MEDIA AND GLOBALIZATION

Terhi Rantanen

SAGE Publications
London ● Thousand Oaks ● New Delhi

First published 2005
Reprinted 2006 (twice)

SAGE Publications Ltd
1 Oliver's Yard
55 City Road
London EC1Y 1SP

SAGE Publications Inc.
2455 Teller Road
Thousand Oaks, California 91320

SAGE Publications India Pvt Ltd
B-42, Panchsheel Enclave
Post Box 4109
New Delhi 110 017

British Library Cataloguing in Publication data

A catalogue record for this book is available from the British Library

ISBN 10 0-7619-7312-5
ISBN 10 0-7619-7313-3 (pbk)
ISBN 13 978-0-7619-7312-6 (hbk)
ISBN 13 978-0-7619-7313-3 (pbk)

Library of Congress Control Number available

Typeset by M Rules
Printed and bound in Great Britain by Athenaeum Press, Gateshead

CONTENTS

LIST OF TABLES

LIST OF FIGURES

Grateful acknowledgement is made to the following sources for permission to reproduce the following material in this book:

Nechemya Orgad © Figures 2.6b, 2.7, 2.8, 3.8, 3.9, 3.10, 4.4, 4.5, 5.3
Sean Song © Figures 2.4, 2.5, 2.6a, 3.6, 3.7, 4.3, 5.2, 6.2

LIST OF MAPS

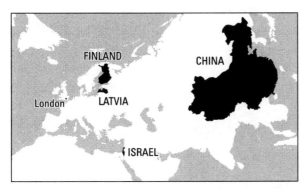

London, Finland, Latvia, Israel and China on the World Map

The national borders on this map as well as others presented in this book are based on the year 2003 and do not reflect frontier disputes.

For the fact was, she could not remember a time when she had not thought of people in terms of groups, nations, or colour of skin first, and as people afterwards.

Doris Lessing (1952)
Martha Quest

1 THEORIZING MEDIA AND GLOBALIZATION

Two words, 'media' and 'globalization', seem to be repeated over and over again. The two go together like a horse and carriage to use a pre-globalization metaphor (we need to decide which comes first), or like a computer and screen to use a high globalization metaphor, although their mutual connection has not always been visible. The early globalization theorist Marshall McLuhan made this connection by combining 'the medium is the message' with his 'global village' (McLuhan and Fiore, 1967), and since then the link between globalization and media has been acknowledged by many, but studied by few. When globalization and media are connected, we also need to know *how* they are connected.

To answer that question, we need to examine what has been done before, even if it has been done separately. Three fields are evident: (1) communication studies; (2) media and cultural studies; and (3) globalization studies. An unfortunate narrowing has to be acknowledged immediately. The influence of Anglo-American academic research is powerful in each of the fields, especially in media and communication studies. Communication studies as a discipline was founded in the USA after World War II and became influential in the 1950s in many countries. British media and cultural studies in the 1970s rose to resist the dominance of US communication studies, found their global niche and became increasingly popular in countries that had earlier imported their communication studies from the USA, especially in Europe (Rantanen, 2000: 38). As a result, most textbooks concentrate on British and US media. The rest of the world often seems invisible because it rarely figures in textbooks written by US and British media scholars.

INTERNATIONAL AND INTERCULTURAL COMMUNICATION STUDIES IN THE UNITED STATES

US communication studies have in general preferred the term 'international communication' rather than 'global media'. International communication studies first emerged in the USA after World War I when it was realized that media and communications played an increasingly important role in war as a consequence of rapidly developing electronic communication (see, for example, Mowlana, 1997: 51–3). In the early days, international communication studies saw the potentiality of media in shaping people's behaviour and attitudes through propaganda. Later, when the field was established after World War II as a subfield of communication studies, it became primarily interested in institutions. International communication grew out of international relations studies that were mainly, as the name indicates, interested in relations between nations. In addition to 'international communication', several terms were used to describe the emerging field such as 'international political communication', 'international propaganda' and 'psychological warfare'. As Mowlana (1997: 3) observes, these three different approaches to international relations share five commonalities:

1   They have a power-driven notion of international relations which is either political or economic or both.
2   They believe in the notion of nation-state as a 'political' state.
3   They make communication and cultural factors subservient to political, economic and technological superstructures.
4   They tend to classify international relations with natural and biological science.
5   They tend to measure what is measurable, observable and tangible.

In practice these also meant that international communication was associated with warfare, diplomatic relations and international organizations. Merrill and Fischer (1970: 126) defined five areas of international communication: (1) the theory of international communication; (2) a descriptive-comparative approach; (3) the role of mass media in national development; (4) the methods of international news reporting; and (5) intergovernmental and financial international communication. As is easily seen from any of the definitions, the intellectual roots of international communication were in the relations between national governments and international organizations.

If the first generation of scholars saw international communication as international relations, the second generation paid attention to the imbalance in these relations. Many scholars described the relationship as media imperialism. The second generation added uneven power relations to the first generation's conceptualization, but left the relationship between nations intact: it was still *international* (between nations or countries) communication.

International communication's negligence of people resulted in the foundation of intercultural communication as a sub-discipline, again in the United States. Intercultural communication includes 'interpersonal communication between members of different cultures, races and ethnic groups' (Asante and Gudykunst, 1989: 9), leaving aside media as institutions and thus the questions of political and financial power. Hence on the one hand there was international communication that was interested almost solely in the media, and on the other hand there was intercultural communication that was mainly interested in people. What was common to both international and intercultural communication was that neither of them paid enough attention to how people used media. Both were trapped in defending their own positions against each other and thus missed the big picture of emerging globalization in which media and communications played a pivotal role in people's experience. The two also missed mediated interpersonal communication (Cathcart and Gumpert, 1986: 27–9) – how media and interpersonal communication become interwoven.

MEDIA AND CULTURAL STUDIES IN EUROPE

As in the United States, British media studies have concentrated mainly on the role of media *institutions* in the process of globalization (see, for example, Golding and Harris, 1997; Boyd-Barrett and Rantanen, 1998; Mohammadi, 1997; Thussu, 1998; 2000). What is also striking is that many media scholars have been eager to show that there is nothing new in globalization, thus rejecting the whole concept instead of contributing to the theoretical discussion on globalization. For writers like Boyd-Barrett (1998: 3) or Sparks (1998: 122) globalization is 'a flawed conceptual tool', or the 'global public sphere should be replaced by the term imperialist, private sphere'. The level of analysis again emphasizes communications structures rather than individual experience and repeats earlier conceptualizations about international relations.

The frustration of not overcoming the division between big and powerful media and what people actually *do* with them gave rise to the birth of cultural studies in Europe and in the United States. Cultural studies differed from media studies in much the same way as intercultural communication differed from international communication. As Servaes (2000: 314) observes, cultural studies cannot be seen as either media- or audience-centred, but instead tends to consider the whole process of communication as a cultural process. Unlike media studies, cultural studies concentrated on the broader issues of culture instead of media. They were also the first to acknowledge the heterogenizing consequences of globalization. It is very much to the credit of cultural studies that these issues were brought onto the agenda. Lull (2000), for example, explicitly refers to the heterogeneous, constantly changing cultural positions and practices without actually mentioning the media. For Lull, globalization

is best considered a complex set of interacting and often countervailing human, material, and symbolic flows that lead to diverse, heterogeneous cultural positionings and practices, which persistently and variously modify established sectors of social, political and cultural power. (2000: 150)

What cultural studies missed, as did intercultural communication, was the media. Cultural studies concentrated mainly on culture as a whole, although they acknowledged the role of people.

GLOBALIZATION STUDIES

Studies on globalization started to emerge in the early 1990s in different fields, but mainly in sociology and geography, of which the latter will be further explored in Chapter 3. However, when social scientists started to talk about globalization in the early 1990s (see, for example, Robertson, 1990; Giddens, 1990), something was missing. Most theorists agree that there is practically no globalization without media and communications, as many of the definitions of globalization at least indirectly acknowledge. Yet ironically it was not media and communications scholars who either started the debate or actively contributed to it. The role of media and communications is, of course, obvious in globalization theories, but it is not necessarily visible. This causes problems in two ways. First, the role of media and communications in globalization theories remains vague and unspecified. Secondly, media studies missed the 'big picture' of globalization and have been contributing little to theoretical discussions on globalization.

Three Phases of Globalization

Giddens talks about three different phases in the current debate on globalization.[1] The first phase witnessed a debate on whether globalization actually existed at all. However, according to Giddens, after the first phase was over, we entered a second phase in which we asked no longer whether globalization existed but what were its *consequences*. Now we are moving toward the third phase of the globalization debate: the response necessary to address the negative consequences of globalization. Before examining those consequences, we need to look at the different definitions of globalization.

Many scholars, including Waters (1995) and Held et al. (1999), have divided the theories of globalization into political, economic and cultural globalization and then conceptualized them accordingly. The problem with this kind of analysis is that when we concentrate on the role of media and communications in globalization they become marginalized in one of the sub-groups, culture, which receives the least attention from scholars outside media studies.

However, media and communications are not merely culture. If we look at Waters's definitions of the three arenas of social life – the economy, the polity and culture – we can see that it is almost impossible to limit media and communications to culture only. For example, according to Waters, the economy consists of 'social arrangements for the production, exchange, distribution and consumption of goods and tangible services', and culture is 'social arrangements for the production, exchange and expression of symbols that represent facts, affects, meanings, beliefs, preferences, tastes and values' (1995: 7–8). It is easy to see that media and communications can be part of both, since it is also difficult to separate media and communications from the polity. We can refer to their increasing role in politics, which has become more and more mediated, and also to their role in the practices of authority, diplomacy and nation-building.

Since the purpose of this book is to concentrate on globalization and media at large, it is too restricting to concentrate merely on the theories of cultural globalization. Most globalization theorists, when they talk about media and communications, neatly pack them together with cultural theories on globalization and rate them secondary to the theories of political and economic globalization. However, if the starting point is the key role played by media and communications in the process of globalization, it is important to look at the general theories of globalization, whether political, economic or cultural, and see the ways media and communications are present in them, directly or indirectly.

A second unavoidable question is the nature of these different theories. Although Giddens suggests that we can separate the three stages of discourse from each other – the first on globalization, the second on its consequences, and the third on what we can do with them – I argue that the consequences have already been embedded in almost every conceptualization of globalization, either explicitly or implicitly. This is why it is impossible to separate the three stages from each other, because when we discuss whether globalization exists, we in fact discuss its consequences and what we should do about them. This is exactly the reason why even the concept of globalization has been so frequently attacked.

Held et al. (1999: 2–10) have distinguished three broad schools of thought among globalization theorists: the hyperglobalizers, the sceptics and the transformalists. The hyperglobalizers consist of theorists such as Ohmae (1995) who predict the end of traditional nation-states. The sceptics such as Hirst and Thompson (1996) claim that globalization is a myth, and that it is only about a heightened level of national economies. The transformation theorists such as Giddens (1990) and Castells (1996) argue that globalization is 'a central driving force behind the rapid social, political and economic changes that are reshaping modern societies and world order' Held et al. (1999: 7).

Not surprisingly, culture, or media and communications, have no notable role in any of the schools. Held et al. (1999: 10) refer to the role of technology and the pop music artist Madonna with hyperglobalists, but otherwise media and communications are simply not present in these schools. Media and communications scholars can criticize themselves for making it easy for scholars from other fields to ignore them, but political scientists and economists should take more seriously the role of media and communications to which they themselves directly refer. For example, Held et al. (1999: 17) provide a framework of four spatio-temporal dimensions which they think provide the basis for both quantitative and qualitative assessment of historical patterns of globalization: (1) the extensity of global networks; (2) the intensity of global interconnectedness; (3) the velocity of global flows; and (4) the impact propensity of global interconnectedness. In each of these categories, as we shall later see, media and communications play a major role. However, they have not received the analysis they deserve.

Definitions of Globalization

Even if we are dissatisfied with the way media and communications have been analysed previously in globalization theories, the starting point has to be the acknowledgment of these theories and a critical evaluation of their value in analysing media and globalization. I have chosen these definitions of globalization particularly for this purpose, and by doing so I inevitably concentrate only on some conceptualizations.

What is striking about the definitions of globalization is that they do not make a distinction between defining the phenomenon itself and its consequences. When we look at different definitions of globalization, we see both. As a result, it is difficult to separate the consequences and the causes of globalization. One of the most 'neutral' definitions is by Giddens, who as early as 1990 defined globalization

> as the intensification of world-wide social relations, which link distant localities in such a way that local happenings are shaped by events occurring many miles away and vice versa. (1990: 64)

But even in this definition Giddens already refers to the consequences: how local happenings are shaped by events many miles away. What Giddens does not say is *how* these happenings are shaped; rather, he emphasizes the *intensification* of worldwide social relations. Although he does not mention media and communications, it is obvious that the worldwide social relations are intensified by them and thus become mostly *mediated*.

Thompson (1995), who focuses more on media and culture than Giddens, is more explicit about the role of media and communications, although like Giddens he does not mention them specifically. He writes:

Globalization . . . refers to the growing interconnectedness of different parts of the world, a process which gives rise to complex forms of interaction and interdependency. (1995: 149)

For Thompson the consequences of globalization are complex forms of interaction and interdependency. He, like Giddens, does not specify what kinds of forms emerge, but implies that they are complex. Thompson's and Giddens's approaches are very similar to each other: both define globalization without specifying homogenization or heterogenization. Compared with Robertson (1992), another early pioneer, the difference is remarkable. Robertson writes that:

Globalization as a concept refers both to the compression of the world and the intensification of consciousness of the world as a whole. (1992: 8)

For Giddens globalization was intensification of social relations; for Thompson it was interaction and dependency; but for Robertson it was the intensification of consciousness of the world as a whole. In this sense, Robertson takes a step further by referring to consciousness instead of social relations. Consciousness is already a more intensified experience of globalization. The same view is shared by Waters, for whom

Globalization is a social process in which the constraints of geography on social and cultural arrangements recede and in which people become increasingly aware that they are receding. (1995: 3)

For both Robertson and Waters, this means that people have become aware and conscious of globalization. However, the question of the consequences of awareness and consciousness for the world as a whole remains unanswered. It is only Albrow (1990), another early pioneer, who concludes that peoples of the world are incorporated into a single world society. He writes:

Globalization refers to all those processes by which the peoples of the world are incorporated into a single world society, global society. (1990: 45)

Albrow's definition implies homogenization – an issue that is highly contested by later heterogenization theorists. As Beck writes, 'how far it [world society] exists may therefore . . . be empirically turned into the question of how, and to what extent, people and cultures around the world relate to one another *in their differences*, and to what extent this self-perception of world society is relevant to how they behave' (2000a: 20, my emphasis).

Beck, like Albrow, refers to people's behaviour and to their reflexivity in their own behaviour. Beck refers to the consequences of globalization more clearly than other scholars quoted here earlier, except Lull. For both

Beck and Albrow, the consequences are unpredictable because of their multiple nature. Another feature is that there is no explicit reference to media and communications. Since media and communications are the topic of this book, the definitions available are inadequate in failing to point out their role in the process. However, several terms used in these definitions implicitly refer to them, such as interconnectivity. If we do not suppose that everybody is on the move, increasing interconnectivity is largely due to media and communications. But what does this increasing interconnectivity mean? How do social relations change when they become more intensified as a result of increasing interconnectivity? What happens when people become more interdependent with their consciousness about the world?

Mediated Globalization

As Lo (2002: 75) observes, the term 'mediation' is defined by Williams (1977: 98) as an 'active' process of relations between 'different kinds of being and consciousness' which are inevitably mediated. According to Lo, Williams rejects the notion of 'reflection' and favours the term 'mediation' to account for the complexity of social reality. But he also cautions that 'mediation' denotes 'constitutive' and/or 'constituting' rather than 'intermediary' (1977: 99–100). Lo (2002: 75) argues that by the same logic, we should consider the media as the *constituting* part of the mediation process, rather than as an intermediary between two parties (e.g. the state and the nation, or the people and national identity). Lo also observes that Martin-Barbero uses the term 'mediation' to denote 'the articulation between communication practices and social movements and the articulations of different tempos of development with the plurality of cultural matrices' (1993: 188). Thus, following Martin Barbero's definition, we need to take into account not only different timing but also different translations in the Silverstone (1999: 21) sense of mediation. Once the unit of our analysis becomes the whole wide world, mediation becomes a much more complex term both temporally and spatially.

Thompson (1995: 149) refers to the *globalization of communication* by pointing out that one of the salient features of communication in the modern world is that it takes place on a scale that is increasingly global. Consequently, we could refer to *mediated globalization* by pointing out that one of the salient features of globalization in the modern world is that it takes place increasingly through media and communications. Hence, we can bring the role of media and communication into the process of globalization by referring explicitly to them. To be able to do this, I define globalization as follows:

> Globalization is a process in which worldwide economic, political, cultural and social relations have become increasingly mediated across time and space.

By highlighting the role of media and communications, I also narrow the definition down. This does not mean that they are the only things that matter. Rather it is because instead of talking about globalization in general, this book concentrates on media and communications and on how people use them world-wide. Concomitantly, it has to ask questions that globalization theorists do not have to ask because they do not refer to the specific role of media and communications. We need to ask Giddens's second and third questions about the nature of the consequences of globalization and what we can do about them when we refer exclusively to media and communications. We also need to ask the question posed by Thompson (1995): 'How do the developments of media and communications affect traditional patterns of social interaction?' He writes:

> The development of new media and communications does not consist simply in the establishment of new networks for the transmission of information between individuals whose basic social relationship remains intact. Rather, the development of media and communications creates *new* forms of action and interaction and new kinds of social relationships – forms that are different from the kind of face-to-face interaction which has prevailed for most of human history. (1995: 81)

Thompson (1995: 81–118) further defines three types of interaction; (1) face-to-face interaction; (2) mediated interaction; and (3) mediated quasi-interaction. For him, face-to-face interaction takes place in a context of co-presence, is dialogical in character, involves a two-way flow of information, and participants employ a multiplicity of symbolic cues. His mediated interaction category includes writing letters and telephone conversations. They already stretch across space and time, which implies that they already contribute to globalization. According to Thompson, the consequence of mediated interaction is ambiguity. His third category – mediated quasi-interaction – is based on social relations established by media of mass communications. It differs in two key respects from both face-to-face interaction and mediated interaction. First, in face-to-face interaction participants are oriented towards specific others for whom they produce actions and utterances, but in mediated quasi-interaction symbolic forms are produced for an indefinite range of potential recipients. Secondly, whereas face-to-face interaction and mediated interaction are dialogical, mediated quasi-interaction is monological in character, in the sense that the flow of communication is predominantly one-way.

If we follow Thompson's own definition, globalization is present in all his categories. However, there is a qualitative change in the nature of interaction when we move from one to the next. By labelling his third category as mediated quasi-interaction he implies that there is a change in the nature of interaction. Instead of being 'real' interaction it actually becomes 'quasi', something imitating the more genuine forms of interaction. By taking this argument further, in relation to globalization, one of the consequences of globalization thus seems to be a mass-experienced monological quasi-interaction, instead of 'real' dialogue.

Tomlinson's (1994) approach is very similar to Thompson's, although he talks not about different modes of communication, but about different modes of experience. His (1994: 50) starting point is Giddens's argument about the experience of the global in the everyday 'situated' lives of people in local circumstances: 'although everybody lives a local life, phenomenal worlds are for the most part truly global' (1991:187). According to Giddens, as a result, modern places are increasingly *phantasmagoric*, since

> locales are thoroughly penetrated by and shaped in terms of social influence quite distant from them. What structures the locale is not simply that which is present on the scene; the 'visible form' of the locale conceals the *distanciated relations*, which determine its nature. (1990: 19, my emphasis)

Hence both Giddens and Thompson seem to indicate that this new experience, when 'social relations are disembedded from local contexts of interaction and their structuring across indefinite spans of time–space' (Giddens 1990: 21), is somewhat different from local experience. In Giddens's case it may even be illusory but it does cause changes in local life. Tomlinson (1994: 153) observes that Giddens defines globalization in terms of distanciation ('the intersection of presence and absence, the interlacing of social relations "at distance" with local contextualities'). As a consequence, according to Tomlinson, it does make sense to think of distanciation as a process of virtual globalization. So here is one of the paradoxes of mediated globalization: at the same time as it connects people, it also distanciates them.

Tomlinson asks what is the nature of this experience. He makes a distinction between mass-mediated and non-mass-mediated experience (1994: 165). While the former is about global experience, the latter is about local experience. According to him there are at least three differences between local and global experience, and correspondingly (although his approach is different from Thomson's) between mediated and non-mediated communication. The first distinction is in terms of scale, although Tomlinson does not see this as crucial since, as Anderson (1983) pointed out earlier, there is the possibility of a sense of community between millions of fellow nationals who never meet each other. The second difference lies in the dispersed nature of mass-mediated experiences of global community compared with those of local community. Here Tomlinson refers to the absence of a history of global experiences compared with experiences of national and diasporic communities. His final distinction is in the nature of mass-mediated communication.

Tomlinson's analysis is very similar to that of Thompson, who claims that mediated quasi-interaction is for the most part monological rather than dialogical. Tomlinson's overall conclusion is that the media audience remains an audience rather than a community. Hence, Tomlinson seems to think that there is a change in the nature of experience; Thompson also thinks that a change in the nature of interaction takes place.

The three approaches by Thompson, Giddens and Tomlinson have similarities as well dissimilarities. They all agree that globalization changes people's lives. For Giddens, globalization changes people's social relations. For Thompson, it changes forms of interaction. Of these three thinkers, Tomlinson is the most optimistic, because for him globalization changes experience. What is evident is that they all think that these three phenomena – social relations, forms of interaction and experience – are interrelated and even overlapping. They also agree that media and communications play an important part in all of them, and moreover that the nature of these relationships is fundamentally changed, largely because of media and communications.

Their conclusions are surprisingly pessimistic, especially if we consider how they all define globalization. For Giddens, Thompson, and Tomlinson globalization is intensification caused by interconnectivity. However, the result of interconnectivity is distanciation, quasi-interaction and monological mass-mediated experience. Both Tomlinson and Thompson agree that the crucial difference is between mediated or non-mediated interaction/experience.

If we agree with these theorists, globalization results in experiences that are mass-mediated and thus not as 'real' or as good as dialogical non-mediated interactive experiences. Hence, as a result of globalization there is a clear shift in the nature of social relationships. Close, intimate and thus genuine relationships are being replaced by new mass-mediated experiences. But is this what mediation does? Are media and the process of mediation so powerful?

This book explores the question of mediated globalization and its consequences. If the role of media and communication is not only acknowledged but also explored, what are the consequences of globalization? Although the starting point of this book is the acknowledgement of media and communications in the process of globalization, it does not claim that they are the only processes that matter. As many globalization theorists have observed, the term 'connectivity' encapsulates many of the characteristics of our age. But it would be too simple to think that media just connect (as mobile phone companies advertise); rather they mediate, which is a much more complex process that involves individuals and their activities and practices. To analyse this complicated process a methodology has to be developed that takes into account the different aspects of globalization, but at the same time acknowledges the role of media and communications.

NEW METHODOLOGY IS NEEDED TO STUDY MEDIATED GLOBALIZATION

How do we study mediated globalization across time and space? To be able to carry out a historical micro–macro analysis, one has to understand the focus of research. According to Giddens,[2] the theory of structuration states that the basic domain of social science study is neither the experience of the individual, nor the existence of any form of societal totality, but *social practices*. Through social activities, people reproduce the actions that make these practices possible. What Giddens is saying, if I read him correctly, is that it is not only the experiences of the individual but also her/his social activities that produce social practices. It is not entirely clear what is the difference between activities and practices, but practices can be seen as repeated activities that have become a pattern. Hence, we can say that media and communications practices are essential in the process of which the outcome is mediated globalization. What we need to do is to find ways to study them.

Just as previous literature offered little on how to theorize this phenomenon, so it also lacked advice on how to develop methodology. International communication was not interested in people; intercultural communication was only interested in people; globalization studies did not study media; and cultural studies mainly studied people in one location and not media. Where should one turn to develop methodology that takes into account global awareness and experiences?

Not surprisingly anthropologists, like media and communication scholars, have encountered the same problem of how to explore micro-worlds with reference to an encompassing macro-world – the system (Marcus, 1998: 33). As Lash and Urry (1987) have observed, major processes such as capitalism are no longer place-bound (Marcus, 1998: 49). The challenge, according to Marcus (1998: 50), is to develop an ethnography that not only collapses the macro–micro distinction, but also focuses on *places* rather than *place*. This is especially true with the process of globalization, since the whole idea behind the concept is its connectivity – the ability to reach beyond one's own place.

INTRODUCING MEDIAGRAPHIES

Thus we approached the crossroads of mediated globalization along the different paths of communication, cultural and globalization studies, and concluded that none of them was theoretically adequate to study the complexity of the phenomenon. What do we do when mediated globalization takes place at different tempos in different places around the world? How do we study it? Clearly, there is a need to develop new methodology to study mediated globalization, taking into account the specifications of media and communication.

The methodology I propose in this book is called *global mediagraphy*. For reasons I will discuss later in this chapter, I want to avoid using the term 'ethno', because although this book is about people, it is also about mediation. I want to use a term that expresses the central role played by media and communications in my analysis. In developing global mediagraphy, I have been much influenced by Appadurai's (1990) theory of scapes in the formation of globalization. As Appadurai (1998: 33–6) has shown, globalization consists of the junctures and disjunctures of five scapes: (1) ethnoscape, (2) mediascape, (3) technoscape, (4) financescape and (5) ideoscape. Ethnoscape consists of persons who are on the move: tourists, immigrants, refugees, exiles and guest workers. Technoscape is both mechanical and informational technology that moves at high speeds across various kinds of previously impervious boundaries. Financescape is currency markets, national stock exchanges, and commodity speculations that also move at high speed. Mediascape refers both to the distribution of the electronic capabilities to produce and disseminate information and to the images created by these media. Ideoscape is composed of elements of the Enlightenment world view, which consists of ideas, terms and images, including freedom, welfare, rights, sovereignty, representation and democracy.

Appadurai writes:

> The suffix -scape allows us to point to the fluid, irregular shapes of these landscapes, shapes that characterise international capital as deeply as they do international clothing styles. These terms, with the common suffix -scape, also indicate that these are not objectively given relations that look the same from every angle of vision but, rather, that they are deeply perspectival constructs, inflected by the historical, linguistic, and political situatedness of different sorts of actors: nation-states, multinationals, diasporic communities, as well as sub-national groupings and movements (whether religious, political, or economic), and even intimate face-to-face groups, such as villages, neighbourhoods and families. Indeed, the individual actor is the last locus of this perspectival set of landscapes, for these landscapes are eventually navigated by agents who both experience and constitute larger formations, in part from their own sense of what these landscapes can offer. (1998: 33)

Although Appadurai seems to think that the individual actor is the last locus of sets, my starting point is exactly the opposite. The aim is to analyse how the lives of individuals in different locations have changed over some 100 years from 1890 to 2003, from Robertson's take-off stage of globalization (see Chapter 2) to today's antagonism. The scapes which Appadurai introduced are present in the analysis, but within an individual interpretation. I do not claim that these changes are universal – there are specific national and local circumstances – but nevertheless similar changes can be found, with different characteristics and timing, around the world.

Appadurai's approach seems to be well suited for the purposes of this book: to study four generations of three families and their mediated globalization. What I like about his approach is its open-endedness: it provides a framework to study globalization, but does not predict its consequences. Appadurai (1998: 31) also refers to imagined worlds, the multiple worlds that are constituted by the historically situated imaginations of persons and groups around the world, thus again emphasizing individuals' capabilities to go beyond what exists even if they physically remain where they are.

I needed methodology that would be sensitive to a mediated globalization that operates in different places rather than in one place. However, place should not be the primary object of the study of mediated globalization. Mediation is something that happens between people in different places. As Marcus puts it:

> For ethnography, then, there is no global in the local–global contrast now so frequently evoked. The global is an emergent dimension of arguing about the connection among sites in a multi-sited ethnography. (1998: 83)

The key word for ethnographers as well as for the purpose of this book is 'multi-sitedness'. According to Marcus (1998: 87), media studies have been one important arena in which multi-sited ethnographic research has emerged. He mentions research on media production and reception as an example. However, the project of this book is different, since it studies not how people relate to specific media texts, but how they connect or disconnect with each other via media and communications. In this way, we do not have the 'macro' system on the one hand and the 'micro' people on the other, but the 'macro' and the 'micro' coming together in people's activities when they use media and communication and thus contribute to globalization.

Saukko (2003: 270–1) defines multi-sited ethnography when research looks at a phenomenon from different locations – at how different sites are connected with and disconnected from each other by diverse flows. The task, according to Saukko, is to do justice to differences and to point to unities that exist across differences. The challenge of conducting this kind of research is that we need to find methodology that is at the same time attentive to similarities and to differences. An additional challenge to the study of mediated globalization is that it is not about people in actual sites, but about 'participants' imaginations that connect them to the global' (Burawoy, 2000: 4). I find Burawoy's observation also extremely important in the context of this book. This is another level that has been previously ignored. People imagine other places, real or unreal, without moving. One can be somewhere physically, but one's mind can travel to other places.

Since the focus of this book is on media and communications and how people use them globally, methods such as ethnography are not sufficient, especially when we want to study processes that go beyond one generation and do not necessarily take place simultaneously in different parts of the world (we are dealing with multiple ethnos in multiple sites). The process of globalization is often uneven not only in resources but also in time. A methodology for the study of mediated globalization should be sensitive to time, which regrettably is not the case with most of media, communications and cultural studies research.

The methodology I am suggesting here is to incorporate individuals and their media use in a structured way into a phenomenon we can call mediated globalization. What I am after is to analyse the individual life histories of four generations of families in different locations that have been previously conceptualized primarily either nationally or individually. It is an attempt to study methodologically the phenomenon of what Beck (2000a: 73) calls the *globalization of biography*, in which oppositions occur not only in the world but also at the centre of people's lives. Its goal is not only 'globalization *from within* the national societies', as Beck (2002: 24) puts it, but globalization that goes beyond national societies. The idea is to relate one life history with others, not only within one family or within one national society but within three families in many locations, and to see what the differences and similarities are. Although the starting point is one person, the aim is to locate his/her story in a wider context and to develop categories for comparison.

Since we are talking about mediated globalization, even methodology is mediated. This sounds self-evident, since it always is (for example, by language), but it deserves further attention. It is perfectly sensible – and this is what anthropologists would probably do – to do ethnographic research in these places. However, my first goal is not to do research on places or countries, because places and countries are no longer the only determining factors. I am primarily interested in mediation, and thus ethnography, even global, can offer us insights but cannot be the only methodology.

MATERIALS AND METHODS

The study uses the materials and methods shown in Table 1.1. As is easily seen from the table, and from the fact that the case studies consist of three families of four generations around the world, there is no way we can research them all in a similar way. For example, in the case of those family members who have already died, surviving members have been interviewed. In two families, the youngest members (the fourth generation) have interviewed their parents and grandparents. In one family, the third generation has interviewed both the previous (the second) and the next (the fourth) generation. Each of the ways of collecting materials has been influenced by various degrees of mediation. The starting point is, in the true sense of Williams (1980: 64–6), the belief that it is difficult to understand the structure of feeling of those generations. This does not however mean that we should not try to achieve the best we can.

TABLE 1.1 Materials and methods

Material	Method
Oral tradition (memories, family histories)	Historical research, interviewing
(Auto)biographies	Self- and comparative introspection
Behaviour	Reflexive ethnography
Photographs and moments	Self- and comparative reflection

Using a variety of methods, I want to look at the materials from different angles. Rather than working on a flat landscape, I am trying to construct a multi-dimensional cube of materials which can be studied by rotation using different 'fingers'. The cube will change in appearance according to the angle of view. The materials are not similar, and there are voids. For example, we do not have photographs from the older generations of two families, for reasons that become obvious when we analyse their histories.

As Burawoy (2000: 4) observes about global ethnography: to be a global ethnographer is one thing, to do global ethnography is another. He sets four different dimensions to global ethnography (2000: 26–27). They are: (1) the extension of the observer into the world of the participant; (2) the extension of observations over time and space; (3) the extension from micro-processes to macro-forces; and (4) the extension of theory. When he wrote about the necessity of the extension of the observer into the world of the participant he probably did not include the possibility of the observer becoming the participant, as has happened in this project. Three members of the three families are not only observers but also participants and analysts. They have become, as Ellis and Bochner (2000: 741) put it, complete member researchers whose narrative interpretations of autobiographies are set against each other. The issue of self-reflexivity also concerns other members of the families in reflecting on their own experiences and on their relationships to their parents and children. In fact reflexivity, in its true sense, has become one of the outcomes of this project: it has made all its participants more aware of the similarities and differences not only across our families but also across time and space.

The scapes are studied through four generations of the three families. The choice of the three families is at the same time not accidental (as their representatives 'volunteered') and yet accidental. They were all physically connected to each other: three members of these families worked or studied in London in the same institution and were thus in contact with each other on a weekly basis. I am not claiming that they are fully 'representative' of what is going on in the world, but I do not consider that they are unrepresentative. They are connected to each other by accident, because three members met each other in a global city when they were working or studying.

The same concerns the nationality of these families. Traditionally they would have been labelled by their nationality, but that would be far from adequate to describe them. When we research on globalization, it is very difficult, if not impossible, to follow the criteria set by the traditional social science (quantitative) idea of comparative research based on people's nationalities. How can one take a representative sample of the 6.5 billion people on the planet? Earlier researchers tried to achieve this using national sampling (20 per cent of Swedes compared with 19.9 per cent of Russians say X), but the globalization debate has already challenged the traditional conceptualization of nations as the point of departure (Robertson, 1990: 25–6) and as representative of homogeneous thinking inside one nation. We need simply to accept the idea that it has become extremely difficult to produce 'representative' material. The more we do research, the more we know about similarities and differences between people that do not necessarily follow the borders of nation-states. We can say that any family's story is typical and atypical at the same time. The main thing is its relationships to other stories and how we analyse them.

CONCLUSION

A consideration of the role of media and communications is highly important for the whole concept of globalization, but in theoretical debates these fields are largely ignored. The blindingly obvious point that there is no globalization without media has not been articulated or analysed clearly enough. The role of media and communications is often reduced either to an exclusively and self-evidently technological one, or to individuals' experiences that are unconnected to the media industries. Nevertheless, the two approaches are not mutually exclusive, because the production of media and the experience of them are linked, often in highly subtle ways.

There is little theoretical interaction between globalization and media scholars. On the one hand, most globalization theorists come from outside media and communication studies and have not studied media *per se*. On the other hand, most media scholars themselves have been occupied mainly with media economy and questions of power and inequality, as numerous books on international communication show. These issues are important, but are not the only ones: globalization theorists have raised many issues (such as the changing concepts of time and space) which cannot be reduced solely to questions of economy and which most international communication scholars have ignored.

The purpose of this book is threefold: to study globalization, media and people. Its aim is to bring together people and globalization and to show the pivotal role played by the media in the process of globalization. Although it is concerned with media and globalization, it does not claim that media and communications are the only things that matter. The idea developed is that individuals, through their individual media activities, which become social practices, contribute to globalization. For this purpose, it introduces a new methodology, global mediagraphy, for researching the role of individuals in mediated globalization.

NOTES

1 http://www.lse.ac.uk/cgi-bin/cached, 21 October 2002.
2 http://www.lse.ac.uk/collections/meetthedirector/faqs.htm#Structuration, 20 September 2002.

2 A HISTORY OF MEDIATED GLOBALIZATION

The first question we need to tackle is the timing of globalization. If we want to study globalization through time and space, we cannot take for granted that globalization started everywhere at the same time and in a similar way. So far much of the general discussion on timing has focused on the relationship between globalization and modernity. The arguments have mainly been about the order of things: what comes first, globalization or modernity? Waters (1995: 4) sees three possibilities: (1) globalization has been under way since the dawn of history; (2) its effects have increased since that time; but (3) there has been a sudden recent acceleration.

THE ADVENT OF GLOBALIZATION

Globalization as a Pre-Modern Project

Although Robertson (1992: 20) sees globalization as a relatively recent phenomenon intimately related to modernity and modernization, as well as to postmodernity and postmodernization, he presents five stages of globalization, going back to the fourteenth century, to 'indicate the major constraining tendencies which have been operating in relatively recent history as far as world order and the compression of the world in our time are concerned' (1992: 26–7). Table 2.1 is based on his analysis, complemented by that of Waters (1995: 43–5). Since Robertson's influential article dates from 1992, I have added a more recent stage of globalization, which I have named the era of antagonism.

The great merit of Robertson's macro-level analysis is that he shows how globalization has accelerated since the fourteenth century and how the necessary components have developed since that time. He also shows how controversial globalization is: it is not good or bad, but includes conflicting and destructive elements that neither go hand in hand with more positive ones nor follow them sequentially. The problem with this kind of periodization, however, is that it is difficult to find support for the argument that media and communications have played a crucial role in globalization, even if Robertson occasionally refers to them. In the absence of information concerning media and communications, we may even ask whether globalization existed before 1875 (this is the argument that has most often been raised against globalization) and whether we need media and communications at all when we talk about globalization, since they are

TABLE 2.1 Six stages of globalization

	1400 to 1750s Germinal	1750s to 1870s Incipient (mainly in Europe)	1875 to mid-1920s Take-off	Early 1920s to mid-1960s Struggle for hegemony	1969 to early 1990s Uncertainty	Late 1990s Antagonism
Agents	Roman Catholic Church Incipient growth of national communities and of state systems downplaying the medieval 'transnational' system	States Sharp increase in conventions and agencies concerned with international and transnational regulation and communication	League of Nations Rise of ecumenical movement Development of global competitions, Olympics, Nobel prizes	United Nations	Number of global institutions and movements greatly increases International system more fluid: end of bipolarity	WTO USA Kyoto Global media Anti-globalization movements Fundamentalist movements
Conflicts			World War I	Disputes and wars about the fragile terms of the globalization process established by the end of the take-off period, World-wide international conflicts concerning form of life	End of Cold War. Societies increasingly face problems of multiculturalism and polyethnicity.	Regional conflicts and genocides Anti-globalization demonstrations Terrorism Wars that include major Western powers but are not fought in their territories

TABLE 2.1 *cont.*

	1400 to 1750s Germinal	1750s to 1870s Incipient (mainly in Europe)	1875 to mid-1920s Take-off	Early 1920s to mid-1960s Struggle for hegemony	1969 to early 1990s Uncertainty	Late 1990s Antagonism
Ideas	Accentuation of concepts of the individual and of ideas about humanity Heliocentric theory of the world	Sharp shift towards the idea of the homogeneous, unitary state Crystallization of conceptions of formalized international relations, of standardized citizenly individuals A more concrete conception of humankind Thematization of the issue of nationalism versus internationalism	Increasingly global conceptions as the 'correct outline' of an acceptable national society Thematization of national and personal identities International formalization and attempted implementation of ideas about humanity	Nature and prospects for humanity sharply focused by Holocaust and atomic bomb	Heightening of global consciousness Accentuation of 'postmaterialist' values in late 1960s Conceptions of individuals rendered more complex by gender, ethnic and racial considerations Civil rights Concern with humankind as a species-community greatly enhanced Interest in world civil society and world citizenship Consolidation of global mass media	Globalization Capitalism Cosmopolitanism Anti-globalization Human rights Fundamentalism Nationalism Multiple identities

TABLE 2.1 *cont.*

	1400 to 1750s Germinal	1750s to 1870s Incipient (mainly in Europe)	1875 to mid-1920s Take-off	Early 1920s to mid-1960s Struggle for hegemony	1969 to early 1990s Uncertainty	Late 1990s Antagonism
Inventions	Spread of Gregorian calendar

Beginning of modern geography | | Very sharp increase in number and speed of global forms of communications

Implementation of world time and near-global adoption of Gregorian calendar | Atomic bomb | Spread of nuclear weapons

Moon landing | Internet

Convergence of media |
| Inclusion | | Beginning of the problem of 'admission' of non-European societies to 'international society' | Some non-European societies | | 'Third World' | Post-communist countries |

Source: based on Robertson, 1992; Waters, 1995

only a minor component among many in Robertson's analysis. Robertson's failure to see the role of media and communications is still more surprising given that he acknowledges their significance when he refers to the development of global media as one of the three factors facilitating the shift towards a single world. He writes:

> More precisely, I argue that systematic comprehension of the macro-structuration of world order is essential to the viability of any form of contemporary theory and that such comprehension must involve analytical separation of the factors which have facilitated the shift towards a single world – e.g. the spread of capitalism, western imperialism and the development of a global media system – *from the general and global agency–structure (and/or) cultural theme.* While the theoretical relationship between the two sets of issues is of great importance (and, of course, complex), confrontation of them leads us to all sorts of difficulties and inhibits our ability to come to terms with the basic and shifting terms of the contemporary world order. (1992: 22)

Globalization as a Modern Project

The second option put forward by Waters (1995: 48) is that globalization is contemporary with modernization and the development of capitalism, but that there has been a recent acceleration. Giddens (1990: 55–63) writes that globalization is directly allied to the development of modern societies, industrialization and the accumulation of material resources, and is a continuation of modernity rather than a break with it. He claims that something has fundamentally changed our previous conceptions of the world, and that we need a new concept to analyse this new epoch. Robertson (1992: 8) also refers to a distinctively different stage of globalization when he writes that globalization in our time is qualitatively different from earlier manifestations, in that modernization has accelerated globalization, which has now permeated contemporary consciousness. Again, like most globalization theorists, neither Waters, Giddens nor Robertson explicitly bring media and communications into the picture, although they hint at them with their reference to the birth of modern societies.

Globalization as a Post-modern Project

Waters's third option is that globalization is a recent phenomenon associated with other social processes known as post-industrialization, post-modernization or the disorganization of capitalism. We can also find support for this option from Giddens (1990: 149) when he terms the contemporary period 'high modernity', from which he infers that modernity has moved into a global stage: society has become a 'world society' and the individual is confronted by social institutions that have become global. This again, like his second option, indicates that the media have a role in this process and also complements Robertson's macro-level analysis.

If we are interested in showing *how* media and communications have facilitated globalization, or even in going further and seeing how media and communications have *accelerated* globalization, we need to leave aside the mainstream globalization theorists, whose main interest is not in this area. We need to go back to research that has concentrated on the historical development of media and communications, although it has not necessarily combined this with a focus on the process of globalization.

A HISTORICAL DEVELOPMENT OF MEDIA AND COMMUNICATIONS

Most globalization theorists, when referring to media and communications, show some ignorance of their historical development. This is obvious when we look at, for example, Robertson's five stages (1992: 58–60). He places the birth of electronic communications only in his third period, although the first electronic media began to operate globally in the first half of the nineteenth century. The first electronic medium, the telegraph, followed by the foundation of the first news agencies, dramatically changed the relationship between the present and the absent.

One of the most influential schools in historical studies of media and communications is the medium theory school, which was mainly developed at the University of Toronto in Canada. Its best known figure is without doubt Marshall McLuhan, whose 'medium is the message' somewhat crudely but wittily captures the key idea. As Deibert writes:

> like other medium theorists, McLuhan believed that changes in models of communication have important consequences for society – that there are deep qualitative differences between one communication model and another, differences that are in turn reflected in the nature of communication epochs . . . Medium theory holds that communication is a sphere where the technology involved has an immense significance to the society where it occurs, and perhaps radically affects the concurrent forms of social and economic organization. (1997: 21)

McLuhan's interest was mainly in how different media act as extensions of the human senses, with consequences for both cognition and social organization (Deibert, 1997: 21). In contrast, his fellow Canadian and teacher Harold Innis (1950), long before the current globalization debate, divided the development of media into three different periods: oral, print and electronic. As he saw it, in each of these periods a change took place in relation to the concepts of time and space. He argued that communication systems shape social organizations by structuring temporal and spatial relations. As a result, different communication systems have given rise to different kinds of empire based on knowledge monopolies. Innis's main concern was the bias of communication: whether empires favoured time or space, whether they were space-bound or time-bound. Space-bias (space-binding) media include the printing press and electronic communications, which lead to expansion and to the control of a territory (space). Time-bias (time-binding) media are sustained by oral culture and manuscripts and lead to expansion and to the control of time. In this sense, Innis did not make a distinction between printed and electronic media, since they both contribute to the control of space (Deibert, 1997: 20).

Several authors have taken up Innis's ideas. McLuhan's 'the medium is the message' is derived directly from Innis's periodization and his emphasis on the importance of communications technology to societal changes. McLuhan's contribution is often sniffed at by some academics, but he has played a pioneering role in acknowledging that the change introduced by electronic communication, especially television, cannot be neglected. Other scholars, such as Lowe (1982), have also divided communications technology into different periods. Lowe writes:

> Culture can be conceived of as oral, chirographic, typographic or electronic, in accordance with the communications media which sustain it. Each of these four types of culture organizes and frames knowledge in a quantitatively different manner than the other three. (1982: 2)

Lowe (1982: 1–2) also argues that the perceptual field thus constituted differs from period to period. Perception is thus bounded by three factors: (1) the communications media which frame and facilitate the act of perceiving; (2) the hierarchy of sensing, that is hearing, touching, smelling, tasting and seeing, which structures the subject as an embodied perceiver; and (3) the epistemic presuppositions which order the content of what is perceived. Lowe's approach, like McLuhan's, stresses the influence on individuals, in contrast to that of Innis, whose analysis focuses on the impact on societies of different modes of communication, as does that of Robertson. However, it was McLuhan who was the first to realize the role of electronic media, i.e. television, in globalization when he wrote that:

> Ours is a brand-new world of allatonceness. 'Time' has ceased, 'space' has vanished. We now live in a *global* village . . . a simultaneous happening. We are back in acoustic space. We have begun again to structure the primordial feeling, the tribal emotions from which a few centuries of literacy divorced us. (McLuhan and Fiore, 1967: 63)

McLuhan's merit is to combine media with globalization, although he used the concept of a global village. He, like Innis, also paid attention to the structural changes that take place when we move from one period to the next. Lull (2000: 38) further developed Innis's periodization, since the latter was writing at a time when television had only just been introduced (Innis refers only to radio). Lull defines four different periods – oral, print, electronic and digital – and looks at how communications systems have shaped social organizations in each of these periods. In Table 2.2 I have divided his electronic period into wired and wireless, in order to build a bridge between Robertson's stages, Lull's periods and the four generations of individuals who will be introduced later in this chapter. For the same reasons, I have also added inclusion and control to Lull's periodization.

TABLE 2.2 Six Stages of Media and Communications

	Oral	Script 3100 BC-	Printed 1440s– (Europe)	Wired electronic 1830s–	Wireless electronic 1920s–	Digital 1990s–
Medium		Letters, manuscripts	Calendars, books, newspapers	Telegraph	Radio, television	Computer, Internet
Communication	Interactive	Mainly interactive	One-way	Mainly one-way	Mainly one-way	Two-way
Time	Real time	Delayed	Delayed	Immediate	Immediate	Internet time
Space	Local	Extended local	Local, extended national	Local, national, increasingly international	Local, national, global	Does not matter
Reach	Small audience	Restricted audience	Mass audience	Mega mass audience	Mega mass audience	All audiences
Inclusion		Literate	Literate	Access based on national infrastructure and affordability	Access based on national infrastructure and affordability	Access and affordability based less on national infrastructure
Control		Church, monasteries, courts	Church, courts, printers, bourgeoisie	Governments, companies	Governments, companies	Companies, governments, individuals

Source: modified from Lull, 2000: 38

Table 2.2 gives a much more accurate analysis of the historical development of media and communications. It is important to note, however, that the periods are not mutually exclusive: that is, the beginning of one period does not mean the disappearance of the previous one. They can exist simultaneously, complementing each other. This is most obvious when we refer to oral communication, which has remained a significant form of communication and has not been replaced by any other form. However, the establishment of one form of communication, and especially its social use, sometimes causes a decline in the previous form. A good example is script communication in the printed era, or the telegraph in the era of the Internet. Sometimes the changes are immediate, but more often they take decades, if not centuries. The development of different media is also deeply interconnected. As McLuhan writes:

> This fact, characteristic of all media, means that the content of any medium is always another medium. The content of writing is speech, just as the written word is the content of print, and print is the content of telegraph. (1964: 29)

McLuhan thus indirectly acknowledges the continuity between different periods. Ong (1982) also refers to it by introducing the term *secondary orality* in analysing the changes from one period to the next, which sometimes include 'going back' in time. He writes:

> At the same time, with telephone, radio, television and various kinds of sound tape, electronic technology has brought us into the age of 'secondary orality'. This new orality has striking resemblances to the old in its participatory mystique, in fostering its communal sense, its concentration on the present moment, and even its use of formulas. (1982: 136)

Although Ong was writing a decade before the globalization debate began, he refers to globalization indirectly by saying that 'secondary orality generates a sense for groups immeasurably larger than those of primary oral culture – McLuhan's "global village"'. In the same way, just as Ong sees radio and television as a means of going back to orality, the Internet could be seen as going back to the age of script in electronic form: people *write* messages that are delivered almost as if they were *spoken*. What happens with the introduction of new technology is a change in the scope of media and communications, be it a change in space or in reach.

Table 2.2 shows several factors that are important in relation to globalization. First, the change in media and communications results in changes in the forms of interaction. In the previous chapter I referred to mediated interaction where communication is mainly one-way. As we see from the table, with the introduction of printed communication the relationship had already been changed to one-way communication. Interestingly, the introduction of the Internet again partly restores the secondary interactive form, although this is mediated in comparison with oral communication.

Secondly, the size of the audience was closely interconnected with the form of communication until the introduction of the Internet. The larger the size of the audience, the more one-way the form of communication.

Again, the Internet challenges this and brings in *secondary chirography* that can also be used for two-way communication. It imitates the telegraph, but is different from it, because it does not require somebody to 'do it for you'; the early books and newspapers required literate people to read them for the non-literate, and the telegraph needed operators.

Although other factors will be discussed in more detail later – time and space in Chapter 3, and exclusion and control in Chapter 4 – it is important to note at this point that these, together with the size of the audience and the form of communication, are decisive when discussing media and globalization. These are the forms that change when societies move from one period to the next, and this has resulted in increasing interconnectivity among different societies.

When we look at Table 2.2, we need to ask: which period is the most important in relation to mediated globalization? To be able to answer this question we need to think about the consequences of each of these periods, in relation not only to social organizations but also to individuals. Innis (1950) suggested that the major change is taking place in the relationship between space and time. According to him, this shift brings changes in the world order in the form of emerging or declining communication empires, the US Empire being the most recent in a long chain. For Innis, in contrast to the contemporary understanding of communications history, which often looks no further back than the history of television, the answer was to look at empires since the dawn of history, from Mesopotamia to Rome, which were also the early communication empires. In a way, Innis's analysis is similar to that of Robertson, who traces the ideas of globalization less far back than Innis but further than modernization theorists.

Tempting as it is to go back to the dawn of history, it seems to me that the answer is obvious, especially when we take into account the work done by McLuhan and by globalization theorists such as Giddens. According to this view, the fundamental change began to take place with the introduction of electronic communication, and has been accelerated by the introduction of digital communication. These two stages of communication coincide with the periods of modernity and post- or super-modernity.

COMBINING MACRO AND MICRO

So far I have introduced a macro-approach to globalization and media based on Robertson's and Lull's stages. But how do we research the role of individuals and their media use in different stages of globalization? The length of these periods makes it possible to observe the influence of globalization and media on a micro-level, on individuals whose life spans cross these periods. Robertson and Lull have shown us how structures have developed, but how do individuals and their lives fit into these structures and also contribute to them? As Beck (2002: 17) reminds us, globalization is a *non-linear*, dialectic process in which the global and the local exist not as cultural polarities but as combined and mutually implicating principles.

As suggested in Chapter 1, mediagraphies offer a way to understand how individuals in different locations across time not only are influenced by globalization but also contribute to it. The main purpose of my analysis here is to introduce a micro level that would complement Robertson's and Lull's macro-level analysis. In this chapter, I am mainly interested in the periodization of globalization and how universal it is. Does it happen in every country at the same time? What forms of media and communications does it take? It is time to introduce the members of the three families on which the analysis will be based.

TABLE 2.3 Family 1: structure

	Great-grandmother Tyyne, 1905–87	Grandmother Eila, 1927–	Mother Terhi, 1953–	Son Nyrki, 1976–
Family	Eleven siblings (two died as infants) Father died when Tyyne was 5 Stepfather	Two sisters (one died as an infant)	No siblings Two stepmothers One stepfather	One brother plus two sisters from father's second marriage Two brothers from mother's second marriage One stepmother and one stepfather
Education	4 years + 1 year (professional course in agricultural husbandry)	11 years + 2 years (professional course in journalism, unfinished)	12 years + 18 years	11 years so far
Profession	Peasant, industrial worker, shopkeeper	Journalist	Academic	Printer
Changes in class	From peasantry to petty bourgeoisie	From petty bourgeoisie to middle class	From middle class to professional middle class	From middle class to skilled working class
Media and communication	Books from 1920, newspapers from birth, radio from 1935, magazines from 1938, film from 1936, phone from 1939, television from 1964	Books, newspapers from birth, magazines, radio from early childhood, phone from 1951, television from 1963, video from 1987, computer from 1980 (work), mobile phone from 1994, Internet from 1998	Books, newspapers magazines, radio, phone from birth, television from 1963, record player from 1967, video from 1987, computer from 1990, Internet from 1990, mobile phone from 1996	Books, newspapers magazines, radio, television from birth, video, computer from early childhood, mobile phone from 1996

First generation: Great-Grandmother Tyyne, 1905–87

FIG 2.1 Three generations in Juva: Tyyne, Antti, his mother, Sisko and Eila

MAP 2.1 Juva, Kotka, Lappeenranta and Helsinki

Tyyne, the oldest member of the family, was born in a small village. Tyyne's childhood was hard; she came from a family of 11 children. Her father died of appendicitis when she was 5 years old, in a horse-drawn carriage on the way to the nearest doctor 8 kilometres from their farm. There was no electricity, no running water, and no shoes for children to wear in the summer. She attended school for 4 years, which was twice as long as her future husband. As newly weds, Tyyne and her husband Antti acquired their own farm where they kept two or three cows, a horse, a pig and some poultry. She gave birth to three daughters in the sauna of the remote farm; one died at 10 days old. The family lived isolated from the rest of the world and, for example, the Civil War that divided the newly born nation in 1918 did not come to their village. Although their life was mainly local, they had access to the outside world through a subscription to a local newspaper that came out three times a week.

The fundamental change in their lives took place during the Great Depression in the 1930s, when Tyyne and Antti had to sell their farm and move to work in a paper mill in an industrial town on the southern coast more than 200 kilometres away. It was sometimes known as 'America' among the people of their region. It symbolized new opportunities, as did America, but provided those opportunities to those people who could not make it there. Antti cried secretly in the stable when his horse was sold before their departure. When they moved to the new location, they lost their house and land and were able to rent from the paper mill only one room (kitchen included) for the whole family. But they now had electricity and could listen to the radio, and later see films. When Antti got a new job selling insurance they moved to the centre of the city and had their first telephone installed. Their life was dramatically changed by the war in 1939–45 when Antti spent 4 years at the front before getting injured. Later in their life, Tyyne and Antti became shopkeepers in a working-class neighbourhood. Tyyne was a devoted Lutheran and maintained her strong religious belief until her death.

Second Generation: Grandmother Eila, 1927–

FIG 2.2 Eila at work with her daughter's picture (see p. 81) in Helsinki

Tyyne's and Antti's elder daughter Eila spent her first 5 years at the family farm and can still speak the local dialect. When the family moved to town, Eila started school. She and her sister Sisko were able to go to a secondary school and study longer than their parents did. Her first foreign language at school was German. The family's life was again affected by global events when war broke out in 1939 with a neighbouring country, and their father was drafted. The sisters spent a lot of time with the family's relatives at their farm during the war when their own home town was bombed. After the war Eila wanted to get away from her father, who drank, and from what she felt was the small-town mentality. She interrupted her schooling and began her studies in journalism in the capital in 1946.

Two years later she interrupted those studies and travelled by ship to a western neighbouring country to work as a cleaner and waitress, in order to learn a language that was the second official language in her country but was not spoken by her family. This country represented a paradise for Eila and her countrymen who had recently lost a war and whose economy was oriented to the payment of war debts, with many basic foods and products rationed. Eila encountered wealth she had never seen before, with shops full of products such as oranges and nylon stockings that were not available in her home country. After 6 months she returned and worked as a journalist for more than 40 years, first in small towns, then in the capital and finally until her retirement in her former home town where she now lives.

Third Generation: Mother Terhi, 1953–

Eila's daughter Terhi was born in a small town more than 200 kilometres from the capital, where she moved with her parents at the age of 5. She lost the connection with relatives in the family's previous location and is unable to speak the local dialect. Her parents divorced when she was 6 years old, a year after they had moved to the capital. English was her first foreign language at school, after the second official language of her own country.

As a teenager, Terhi started to listen to foreign pop music on Radio Luxemburg. Every year she also watched the Eurovision song contest, a highly popular programme in her country at that time, although it often got 'zero points' and came last, which was followed by a public debate in the mass media on the reasons why this had happened (usually explained by the difficulty of the language). Through the media she was much influenced by television news films on invasions, famines, wars and *coups d'état* in other parts of the world.

Unlike her parents and grandparents, who were critical of their country's eastern neighbour because of the 1939–45 war, she developed a keen interest in this country, which she frequently visited later as a researcher. She completed all her studies and worked as an academic in the capital, where she also got married and gave birth to her two sons. She divorced when her children were 6 and 3 years old. After her children reached adulthood she moved to a global city, where she now lives with her second husband and teaches in a university.

Fourth Generation: Son Nyrki, 1976–

Terhi's son Nyrki was born in the capital and has lived there all his life. He lived in the same neighbourhood and flat where his grandmother and mother have lived until he was 18 years old. He attended kindergarten from seven months old until he went to a local school. From his early childhood Nyrki has had access to different media and communications and can be identified as a member of a global media generation that has been able to reach a wider world beyond national boundaries. However, Nyrki and his younger brother Sampo strongly identify themselves as natives of their home country and especially of its capital. They both live, study and work in the capital, although Nyrki has also worked in the global city where his mother now lives.

FIG 2.3 Four generations in Helsinki: Eila, Tyyne with the newborn Nyrki, and Terhi

Nyrki and Sampo both reject the choices of their parents. They did not want to study the language of either of their neighbouring countries, preferring English. Neither do they share their parents' belief in education. From their early childhood they have travelled abroad as tourists every year and they also lived in another country for 6 months with their mother. They became interested in rap music during their stay there, and back in the capital they wore black baseball caps for several years. This identified them as *hoppari* (from the word 'hip-hop') and occasionally made them the object of attacks by local skinheads in their home town when they were teenagers. Their adopted sisters from another part of the world (from their father's second marriage) have made them very aware of racism in their culturally homogeneous country.

TABLE 2.4 Family 2: structure

	Great-grandfather Baosheng, 1888–1971	Grandfather Zhansheng, 1923–2000	Father Qinghe, 1944–	Son Junjie, 1974–
Family	Four siblings	Four siblings	Seven siblings	Three siblings
Education	Primary school	3 years primary school	8 years primary school and junior middle school	13 + 4 (undergraduate) + 2 (postgraduate)
Profession	Peasant	Peasant	Peasant, civil servant	Journalist
Changes in class	None (peasantry)	None (peasantry)	From peasantry to middle class (but collective)	None (middle class)
Media and communication	Government loudspeaker installed at home in people's commune in the 1960s, books from 1900s, film from 1950s, radio from 1960s	Books from 1930s, newspaper seldom, radio from 1960s often, magazines seldom, film from 1950s, telephone from 1990s, television from 1980s, computer never	Books from 1940s, newspapers 1950s, radio 1960s, magazines 1950s, film 1950s, phone 1980s, television 1970s, computer and Internet sometimes	Books 1970s, newspapers 1980s, radio 1980s, magazines 1980s, film 1980s, phone 1980s, television 1980s (first private TV set in 1985), computer and Internet 1990s

First Generation: Great-Grandfather Baosheng, 1888–1971

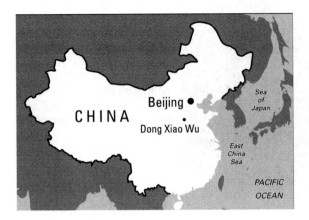

MAP 2.2 Dong Xiao Wu and Beijing

Baosheng primarily lived his life locally, in a relatively isolated village. He studied for a couple of years in the primary school of his village and was always proud of his good calligraphy using a brush. Later he married a woman from his village, and they lived all their life in that same place, where he owned a house and a piece of land before a land reform. Their life was not easy, but Baosheng tried hard to improve the financial status of his family. In addition to the income from his land he earned his living by selling coal. He had few opportunities to travel and little direct access to the modern media, except listening to the radio and watching films shown publicly in the village in the last two decades of his life. Baosheng was deeply religious, an active Taoist who served in the village temple.

His life was changed dramatically because of war. From the early 1930s the north-eastern areas of his country were gradually invaded by foreign troops. They took over Baosheng's village in 1937, the year his son got married at age 15. After the war, in 1945 a civil war followed between the Communist Party and the Nationalist Party. This war ended in the victory of the Communists in 1949.

Second Generation: Grandfather Zhansheng, 1923–2000

Zhansheng, Baosheng's second son, also lived in the same village all his life. His father Baosheng appreciated education and his son was allowed to study for 3 years at school. This was quite important for the family, because Zhansheng got the idea that his children should become intellectuals. During the occupation his father was afraid that the invaders would kill Zhansheng and capture his wife and he hid them in a cave near the village. Zhansheng was lucky and was only forced to construct a railway.

FIG 2.4 Three generations in Dong Xiao Wu: Zhansheng (second row, second from the right) with his wife Chun La (second row, second left) and their children and grandchildren

After the war when land reform started, peasants were divided into four different classes: poor peasants, middle peasants, rich peasants and landlords. Baosheng's and Zhansheng's family belonged to the middle peasants, which meant his family was 'good class' at that time. Rich peasants and landlords were considered 'bad class' and needed to be 'revolutionized'. The reform abolishing the private ownership of land took place between 1949 and 1952, and about 50 per cent of all the arable land was redistributed (Hutchings, 2000: 364–5). Zhansheng supported the reform and gave away his land and property to the newly established people's commune.

After the establishment of the people's commune Zhansheng became, for several years, a leader of one of the eight work groups in their village. Zhansheng had seven children, of whom six attended at least a junior middle school. Later, he travelled to many places to see his children, including another province where his second son was stationed as a soldier, and the capital where his son-in-law was stationed. He relied on the radio and television as major sources of entertainment in later life. The mass media changed some of his traditional views, for example his support for the unequal status of men and women. In his later years he wanted to move to a different county, but he was unable to fulfil his dream. Although he adjusted to the Communist system, he maintained his religious values.

Third Generation: Son Qinghe, 1944–

Zhansheng's son Qinghe resisted his father's religious beliefs and became a committed atheist. Qinghe also became an active supporter of a political leader of his new country, mainly because he was influenced by his socialist ideology. He started life as a peasant in the same village as his father, then became a worker in a brickyard near the village, and finally in the early 1980s became a civil servant in a local government office, while still continuing to work on the family farm. Hence, he could use the opportunities that were available in society to promote his career in a Communist system. Because of his social rise and increased wealth the family was able in 1985 to afford a private television set.

Qinghe's three children all have at least an undergraduate degree. When his eldest daughter, in the early 1980s, was the only one in the whole county to receive an offer to study at a university, it was a sensational event. In his country, only 2 per cent of people have a university degree.

FIG 2.5 Qinghe with his wife Ju Hua in Dong Xiao Wu

His daughter became a role model to her siblings by bringing books and newspapers home and by giving them instruction and encouragement. The family became the only one with all the children studying at university, in a village where most young people were unable to finish their primary schooling.

Fourth Generation: Junjie, 1974–

Junjie spent his childhood in the same village as the previous generations of his family, where his parents looked after him before he went to school. He went to a primary school in the village, to junior middle school in a nearby village and to high school in another county. He went on to university in the capital and did his postgraduate studies in two Western global cities. Junjie moved permanently to the capital after he graduated from university. He could use the opportunities that were emerging after his home country had decided to establish an open door policy towards the Western world. He stayed in the capital for 8 years before moving abroad to study and work.

In Junjie's family, three generations have lived in the same village. Although Qinghe moved to live in a small town, it is only Junjie whose location has dramatically changed from a small village to cosmopolitan cities. He is the first member of the family to live in the capital and abroad.

FIG 2.6a Junjie (left) with his family

FAMILY 3

The structure of family 3 is shown in Table 2.5.

First Generation: Great-Grandfather Moshe, 1881–1941

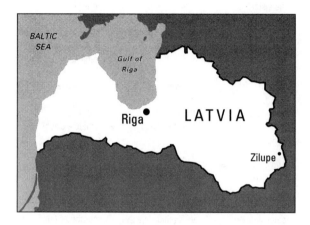

FIG 2.3 Zilupe and Riga

The great-grandfather Moshe was a shopkeeper and a wealthy man. He was also already urban: he lived in a small border town. He belonged to an ethnic minority comprising 7. 4 per cent of the population. He went to a school where children could be educated in their own religion and language. As a result of Moshe's ethnicity and education, but also because of the borderland culture of his home town, he knew four languages.

Moshe was religious and strictly traditional: Saturdays and holidays were observed by closing his shop, he regularly attended the synagogue, and he kept a kosher diet. At the same time, he already had access to modern media and communications. He had a telephone in his shop for business and a gramophone at home for entertainment. He saw his first movie (Charlie Chaplin) at the age of 28 with his children. These films were silent, and often a pianist played music while the film was screened.

When his country became independent in November 1918, Moshe received full citizenship and the right to vote for the first time. After it was invaded in June 1941, he was shot dead while sweeping the pavement in front of his shop. The rest of the family were killed or died in concentration camps.

TABLE 2.5 Family 3: structure

	Great-grandfather Moshe, 1881–1941	Grandfather Lasik, 1912–97	Father Nechemya, 1941–	Daughter Shani, 1972–
Family	Three sisters	Two brothers, one sister	Three brothers	Two brothers, one sister
Education	Jewish education in the 'heder'	12 years high school	12 years high school	12 years high school + 7.5 years higher education (so far)
Profession	Draper	Peasant	Manager	PhD student
Changes in class	None (middle class all his life)	From peasantry to middle class (collective)	None (middle class)	None (middle class)
Media and communication	Books (Russian and Yiddish), religious books, daily newspaper in Yiddish, gramophone, telephone (only for business matters, located in the shop)	Books, newspapers, radio, cinema, television (since age 55), public phone (since age 42), domestic phone (since age 63)	Books, newspapers, radio, cinema, public phone (since age 18), VCR (since age 29), computer and Internet (since age 54) mobile phone (since age 59)	Books, newspapers, radio, cinema, television, VCR (since age 10), computer (since age 20), Internet (since age 23), mobile phone (since age 25)

Second Generation: Grandfather Lasik, 1912–97

Moshe's son's Lasik was much influenced by two important global ideoscapes of that time: Zionism, which promoted the idea of a home country for people like him without a land of their own, and socialism. He left his country of origin following a *coup d'état* in 1934, after which political activity diminished as political parties and many organizations were shut down.[1]

In contrast to his father, Lasik was secular. He became a member of the fifth immigration in the 1930s, which brought 247,000 new immigrants to a 'promised land' (Laqueur, 1972: 320). Lasik chose to live in a labour movement kibbutz. The kibbutz which Lasik chose became the epitome of secularism, promoting a non-religious and even anti-religious lifestyle. He consciously rebelled against everything associated with the religious lifestyle, although he did appreciate values and tradition.

His new ideoscape can also be seen as a revolt against his religious parents who were strongly against their son's decision to leave everything

FIG 2.6b Lasik (upper row, in the middle) with his fellow youth organization members in Zilupe

FIG 2.4 Kinneret and Tel Aviv

behind and emigrate to a new country. Notwithstanding this, his father Moshe supported his son financially and enabled him to join the Aliyah. Lasik's move also included a strong commitment to non-materialistic values, choosing the collective lifestyle of a kibbutz and as a result a decline in wealth. After his departure from the home country he kept contact with his relatives there by mail until their disappearance and death. He himself never returned there, and neither have his children or grandchildren.

Lasik's move meant not only leaving his family and home town: he also left behind his language. The new immigrants adopted a new language instead of their mother tongue. Their mother tongue was associated with their past as an oppressed people with no land. Previously they had known their new spoken language only as a written religious language. Many immigrants also translated their former surnames into the new language or simply adopted new ones.

Lasik resisted electronic media even to the extent that he refused to use the communal media available in the kibbutz. Lasik first got a TV at home only at the age of 55 when televisions were introduced to private homes in the kibbutz. Until then there was a collective television in the kibbutz's communal room.

Third Generation: Father Nechemya, 1941–

Lasik's son Nechemya lived all his childhood in the kibbutz. He was raised in a communal kindergarten and never lived with his parents in their house.

Nechemya slept from birth until he was 18 years old in the communal 'children house'. He recalls one night at his children house, at the age of 7, when one of the girls was screaming in her bed 'Night guard!! Night guard!!' rather than calling her mother or father; she was 'programmed' (as Nechemya puts it) to call the night guard at the children house. The night guard would usually appear within an hour, since she was engaged in patrolling and visiting the other children houses which were dispersed all over the kibbutz.

Nechemya rejected the first language of his parents. For him it connoted diasporic mentality, with which he refused to associate himself. His rejection of their language was embedded in the general atmosphere and education in the kibbutz, which emphasized machismo, the image of the 'Sabres' and the rejection of a diasporic lifestyle. His avoidance of their language was also a way of rebelling against his parents who used it as a 'secret language' when they did not want their children to understand (later, when Nechemya's generation became parents, they would use English as their 'secret language'). Today he regrets his rejection of their language and wishes he knew it.

The first movie Nechemya saw was Disney's *Mickey Mouse*, shown in the kibbutz when he was 5 years old. He first heard recorded music in the kindergarten from an old tape recorder operated by a kind of wire, which was brought by his teacher from abroad. His early media use was very much collective: Nechemya got his first television when he was 24 years old.

After his marriage, Nechemya, his wife and their daughter lived for a

FIG 2.7 Nechemya (in front) with his family on a boat trip to Tiberias

FIG 2.8 Shani with her grandparents Lasik and Batya in an amusement park in Brussels

couple of years in the kibbutz. He, however, decided to leave behind the collective lifestyle of which his father had been a dedicated advocate and to work abroad, if only for 4 years, in the 1970s. The change from a protected and simple way of life in a remote kibbutz to urban life in European cities was difficult for him. Although he returned to his home country, he never went back to live in a kibbutz, but regularly visits it and maintains his identity as a kibbutznik.

Fourth Generation: Daughter Shani, 1972–

Shani was born in the kibbutz and lived there during her early years. She spent her early schooling in a kindergarten like her father. Because of her father's work, Shani lived between the ages of 5 and 9 in two different countries. While abroad she went to a Muslim kindergarten because her parents did not want to her to go to an Orthodox religious kindergarten. She still remembers how children had to take their shoes off and how she was booed for wearing national colours at a performance where children represented different countries.

While living abroad Shani's parents tried to reinforce her national identity by reading her mainly books in her native language, so that she would not forget it. Shani did develop a strong national identity and was surprised, on her family's return to their home country, that her friends did not share this to the same extent. Shani remembers how she watched the Eurovision song contests every year and how much it meant to her when the group Milk and Honey from her home country won in 1979 with the song 'Hallelujah'.

Although Shani's family returned to their home country where she studied and worked, she decided to do her postgraduate studies in a global city where she has now lived for 5 years. She recently got married to a fellow student from her home country and has now got her first job as a university teacher. She has considered staying in this global city at least for a couple of years, but wants to go back to the home country when she starts a family.

CONCLUSION

This chapter has looked at the development of globalization through three different lenses: Robertson's stages of globalization, Lull's periodization of media and communications, and the individual life histories of four generations of three families. While Robertson's analysis explains the major factors in globalization, Lull's analysis contextualizes the media within the process of globalization, and the two are combined here within individual life histories.

What becomes very clear from each mediagraphy is that globalization is an uneven process in which individuals around the world do not necessarily experience the same things at the same time, although their lives bear many similarities. The take-off period from 1875 until the mid 1920s (see Table 2.1) makes the members of the three families citizens instead of subjects. It also marks a period when both Tyyne and Moshe are granted universal suffrage. Hence, the thematization of national and personal identities starts in this period for at least two of the families when they become identified as members of a particular nation-state.

However, if we have a closer look at the individuals, the picture becomes somewhat different. Tyyne and Baosheng both had at that time primarily a local identity as they were very place-bound. Baosheng had no access to the media and communications, and Tyyne was primarily dependent on a local newspaper. Their main form of communication was oral, script (as Baosheng's knowledge of calligraphy shows) and printed (limited for Tyyne). Only Moshe, who was living an urban life, had access to the first electronic media. In this sense, the take-off period had started for Moshe, a city dweller, but not for people like Tyyne and Baosheng who still lived in their villages. Despite the differences in their locations, Tyyne, Baosheng and Moshe were deeply religious, though they believed in different gods. Such global agents as the League of Nations, which Robertson mentions in his periodization, had very little direct impact on their lives.

The phase of the struggle for hegemony from the early 1920s to the mid 1960s again is experienced in similar and different ways. This period was the most dramatic for each of the families, when the family members either lost their life or experienced war for several years or decades. Simultaneously, it is also a period of rising nationalism and of increasing media and communications. This is no coincidence. As Anderson (1983) has argued, nationhood is imagined: it is based on the act of simultaneous newspaper reading among people who would otherwise have never met each other. Anderson argues for the importance of printed media, but broadcasting has also been seen to contribute to nationalism (Scannell, 1989). It is in this period that the members of these families develop a distinctive national identity.

Although the members of these families do not necessarily share ideologies, they are all touched or divided by them. This is the period when ideologies clash: individuals are divided by ideologies such as communism and capitalism, but they are also united by them. It also marks the decreasing importance of religion.

Media and communications start to have an effect on people's lives in the period of uncertainty from the late 1960s until the early 1990s. The world is still divided by the Iron Curtain, but increasingly global media and communications are able to pass through it. More people become more aware of other people at distance, of different ideologies and sets of beliefs. More people start to travel and to use different kinds of media. This is the period when television reaches all three families. The fourth generation, whatever its location, is much influenced by global youth culture.

When compared using the six stages of media and communications (see Table 2.2), all generations have had access to most of them. Obviously, all of them use oral communication in their non-mediated, face-to-face communication in their locations, although not necessarily in their own language. All of them have also been able to use script and printed communication in their mediated interaction. Wired electronic communication has generally affected their lives at least indirectly where telegraph lines have reached their locations. Every member of the family has been able to use wireless electronic communications in the form of radio, and most of them have also wed television. Digital communication, however, is mainly accessible to those members of the families who either can afford it or know how to use it.

The role of a nation-state has been deliberately played down in this chapter. If we had maintained our analysis on a country unit level, we would have missed many of the similarities between the families and probably concentrated more on their dissimilarities, thus missing the big picture of globalization. It is now time to look more closely at both, focusing on the consequences of globalization and how it has changed the lives of these three families.

NOTE

1 http://www.latinst.lv/n_minorities/jews.htm, 22 October 2002.

3 TIME, PLACE AND SPACE

If we agree that modernity and post-modernity are the most important periods for globalization in relation to media and communications (although acknowledging that there were globalizing elements in earlier periods), our next question concerns the outcomes of globalization. One of these, mentioned in passing in Chapter 2, concerns the relationship between time, place and space. We need to ask what happens to time, place and space between one period and the next. To answer this question, we need to go back to globalization theorists who have underlined the importance of an analysis of these concepts. Again we encounter a challenge: how to combine these concepts with individuals, and especially with their use of media and communications.

The introduction of the concepts of time, place and space into discussion on globalization more than 10 years ago marked a clear break with traditional Marxism and can be seen as a general critique of Marxist theory, an attempt to shift the discussion away from purely economic and political issues. This is the reason why, for example, these concepts have never been an issue for the field of international communication, as it has been primarily occupied with economy and politics. As Harvey (1993: 3) writes, traditional Marxism had neglected time, place and space in its analysis of modern societies. Harvey proposed four arenas of development to overcome what he called 'the supposed crisis of historical materialism and Marxism' (1993: 3). Among them was the recognition that the dimensions of time and space matter. According to Harvey, time and space are real geographies of social action, real as well as metaphorical territories and spaces of power; they are the sites of innumerable differences that have to be understood both *in their own right* and within the overall logic of capitalist development.

Much of the theoretical work has been done in geography (see, for example, Harvey, 1990, Massey, 1994), although some social scientists have also picked up issues and developed them further (see, for example, Giddens, 1990; Lash and Urry, 1987). Although each of them approached these concepts from their own angle, there are also issues that they all consider vital for the understanding of globalization. One is the recognition of time, place and space as social constructs, and not as categories to be taken for granted and thus 'natural' and stagnant.

TIME–SPACE DISTANCIATION AND TIME–SPACE COMPRESSION

Harvey and Giddens have used slightly different terms to analyse changes in time, place and space. Giddens (1990) uses the term 'time–space distanciation', while Harvey (1990) talks about 'time–space compression'. Both acknowledge that they are social constructs and that the world is becoming a smaller place owing to technological advances that enable people to interact with one another across the globe.

Giddens (1990: 17–21) writes that in pre-modern contexts both time and space were fundamentally linked to a person's immediate location, but the invention and diffusion of the mechanical clock had the effect of universalizing time. He observes that the liberation of time and space is a prerequisite for globalization as a direct consequence of modernity. Harvey, like Giddens, begins with an analysis of the pre-modern conceptions of time and space, but for him (as a geographer) the issue of space is primary (Waters, 1995: 54). He also writes that time was constituted as a linear and universal process by the invention of the mechanical watch, but it is here, as Waters (1995: 55) remarks, that Harvey's analysis departs from that of Giddens, who portrays time as differentiating from space. Harvey argues that the objectification and universalization of the concepts of time and space allowed time to annihilate space, and that time can be reorganized in such a way as to reduce the constraints of space and vice versa. For Harvey, time–space compression involves a shortening of time and a shrinking of space: the time taken to do things is progressively reduced, and this in turn reduces the experimental distance between different points in space (Waters, 1995: 55).

Waters (1995: 58) notes that Giddens's term 'distanciation' gives the impression that time and space are becoming stretched. He claims that Giddens's intended meaning is not this, but is rather that social relationships are becoming stretched across great distances. Waters here makes an explicit remark about media and communications when he writes that the new communications technologies are ensuring that transglobal social relationships are becoming more intense and robust rather than stretched and attenuated. According to Waters (1995: 58), Harvey's notion of compression of social relationships, rendering spatial distance unimportant, fits the proposal of a globalizing trend far more closely than Giddens's notion of distanciation.

Hence, we have two conflicting views of the consequences of globalization: either global social relationships become stretched as a result of time–space distanciation, or they become more intense and robust as a result of time–space compression. Whichever concept we use – and we will come back to this question later – we are giving attention to a phenomenon that has not hitherto received the attention it deserves. This is important in itself, and the globalization debate has thus added a new dimension to our understanding of the contemporary world.

TIME AND THE MEDIA

The *taming of time*, as Ong (1982: 76) observes, took place with the introduction of calendars and clocks. Calendars set up annual, monthly and weekly time. Many holidays marked in them were based on religious 'holy days' (Zerubavel, 2003: 30), underlining the centrality of religion in societies. With the observance of these holy days, time was structured and organized: the observance of Sundays or the Sabbath are self-evident examples. The calendars were constructed on an annual and weekly cycle, but with mechanical clocks a daily cycle was introduced. As Ong writes:

> Time is seemingly tamed if we treat it spatially on a calendar or the face of a clock, where we can make it appear as divided into separate units next to each other. But this also falsifies time. Real time has no divisions at all, but is uninterruptedly continuous: at midnight yesterday did not click over into today. No one can find the *exact* point of midnight, and if it is not exact, how can it be midnight? (1982: 76)

Unlike Ong, Giddens (1990: 17) sees *the shrinking of time* as starting only with the invention of the mechanical clock. However, even after the introduction of the mechanical clock, every location had its own time. This lasted until time zones were introduced in 1844. Zerubavel viewed the rise of standard time in the context of the establishment of national and international communication networks following the introduction of railway transportation and telegraphic communications. He fully acknowledges the role of communications in this process and writes:

> It was not until the revolution in communication that the situation began to change in any significant way. The indispensability of a uniform standard time that would allow some temporal coordination at supra-local level was a direct product of the establishment of a *national communication network*. (1982: 5)

For Zerubavel, it is the emergence of national communication networks that explains the need to synchronize different communities and countries with one another. He also acknowledges its importance to globalization, writing that 'the validity of . . . the temporal reference framework has already reached the global level' (1982: 5). Zerubavel acknowledges the difference between local and global (standardized) times. He writes:

As late as the mid-19th century, the only valid standard of time was local time. Each city, town, or village had its own time, which applied to it alone. Thus, there was a plurality of local times, which were coordinated with one another, since no locality was concerned with the local times of other localities. (1982: 5)

For Zerubavel (1982: 6–7) the introduction during the 1780s of the British mailcoach service, which ran in accordance with strict schedules, was the first sign of this process of creating national communications networks. However, it was the introduction of railway transportation that promoted the standardization of time reckoning at a supralocal level, by bringing different communities within more immediate reach of one another and thus making people more aware of the fact that the local times of other communities were different from and not coordinated with their own. In Britain in 1840, 15 years after the introduction of the first passenger trains, the Great Western Railway began to use only Greenwich mean time (GMT) throughout its timetables and stations, and was soon followed by other railway companies (1982: 7).

Since in most countries the telegraph was built along railway lines, it makes sense that the next step was that the telegraph also started to use GMT. But this time its effect was more far-reaching: the telegraph was not only a national network but international, connecting different national telegraph networks to each other – as the 'girdle around the world'. It was the telegraph that introduced the new global time. It was also the telegraph that separated a message from its carrier and connected news and time closely to one another. The use of the telegraph signal also made it possible to synchronize local time with GMT. The first international agreement on the standardization of time zones was concluded in 1884, when 25 countries accepted an invitation to participate in the International Meridian Conference held in Washington, DC (1982: 13).

Improved transportation and communications enabled access to events beyond people's own experience. People, of course, were able to travel more easily, but what is even more important is how messages were transported. When newspapers delivered messages, both the gathering and the delivery of news were dependent on transportation. For example, the journey from the east to the west coast of the USA took 2 years on foot, 4 months by stagecoach, but only 4 days by train (Lash and Urry, 1987: 229). As a result of progress in transportation, major changes took place in the relationship between time and space, namely the shrinking of distance in terms of the time taken to move from one location to another (Meyrowitz, 1985: 116).

It is not difficult to discern that the fundamental change in the relationship between time, place and space coincided with the shift from printed to electronic communication. The telegraph, as the new technology that made electronic communication possible, played a crucial role. Carey

(1989: 203), for example, considers the telegraph a watershed in communication. Among other things, it changed the nature of language, of ordinary knowledge, of the very structure of awareness. According to Meyrowitz (1985: 13), the invention and use of the telegraph began to erode the informational differences between different places and to destroy the specialness of place and time.

The telegraph profoundly changed the relationship between news and time because, as Giddens puts it, globalization can be defined as 'the intensification of worldwide social relations which link distant *localities* in such a way that local happenings are shaped by events occurring many miles away and vice versa' (1990: 64, my emphasis). The closer connection between the media and time developed in the process of nineteenth-century news transmission. Of course, news has always been new: that is, something that was not available before. But before the invention of the telegraph, news always needed a carrier and thus travelled only as fast as that carrier. Earlier, before the telegraph, news could be quite dated by the time it was received. At the beginning of the eighteenth century, the minimum transmission time from England to Massachusetts was 48 days. For example, unofficial news of the death of King William in 1702 did not reach his American subjects until almost 3 months later (Stephens, 1989: 220).

The later development of media and communication technology compressed time and space even further. Carey (1989) has examined the role of radio in the invasion of time. According to him (1989: 88), once the spatial frontier was crossed, time became the new frontier. Carey sees first Sunday newspapers and then radio penetrating the sacred time of the Sabbath. Previously, the Sabbath had been free from control by the state and commerce – a time when another dimension of life could be experienced and altered forms of social relationship could occur. With the invention of Sunday newspapers and the radio, this sacred time was lost. Later, the radio evaded time by starting to broadcast 24 hours a day, taking over the last frontier – the night.

Electronic communication and news, first by the telegraph and later by radio, television and the Internet, created a new concept of time that hastened the space of life by constantly reminding people that something was happening – if not here, then somewhere else. Not only do people become aware of other places and the events occurring there, but the media remind them that the world never sleeps even if its audience does.

The role of media in the process of time–space compression is among the consequences of time coordination. Mumford writes:

> One further effect of our closer time co-ordination and our instantaneous communication must be noted here: broken time and broken attention. The difficulties of transport and communication before 1850 automatically acted as a selective screen, which permitted no more stimuli to reach a person than he

could handle: a certain urgency was necessary before one received a call from a long distance or was compelled to make a journey oneself: this condition of slow physical locomotion kept intercourse down to a human scale, and under definitive control. Nowadays this screen has vanished: the remote is as close as the near: the ephemeral is as emphatic as the durable. While the tempo of the day has been quickened by instantaneous communication, the rhythm of the day has been broken: the radio, the telephone, the daily newspaper clamour for attention, and amid the host of stimuli to which people are subjected, it becomes more and more difficult to absorb and cope with any one part of the environment, to say nothing of dealing with it as a whole. (1986: 21)

The media have also created the idea of the mass audience: the same message delivered to many people around the world at the same time. What this meant in practice was that places started to open up to the mediated relationships provided by the mass media. What was earlier considered to be out of reach was now reachable through the media. Something fundamental changed: the places people lived in were no longer the only places they had access to. This change touched both people and places. It is not only that place and space became partly separate from each other, but also that hitherto unknown places began to have an effect on known places. When space shrinks, what is out there becomes closer and brings changes in both people and places.

Time cannot be understood without the concept of place and space. We need to ask: what happens to places and to the experience of places when the world shrinks?

PLACE AND THE MEDIA

Before the modern period, everything that could be reached was in a place. This is what globalization theorists refer to when they claim that in pre-modern times the experience of place overlapped with the experience of time and space. In pre-modern times, everything, including time and space, was in one's place, because one had no knowledge of anything beyond one's own immediate experience.

Although the use of place and space is often overlapping and confusing, it is important to try to distinguish between the two. If people's experience of time, place and space has fundamentally changed, what then is actually changing? To answer this question it is important to differentiate place from space. For Giddens (1990: 18), place is best conceptualized by means of the idea of locale, which refers to the physical settings of social activity as situated geographically. Place compared with space is something familiar and concrete ('there is no place like home'). Relph writes that 'to be human is to live in a world that is filled with significant places and to have and to know your place' (1976: 40). Space is often understood as something bigger than place, often even as something empty. The shrinking of space is equivalent to the shrinking of distance in purely geographical terms. Space is thought to be out there, outside the borders of place. It can also be unknown and unconquered, an open space. In contrast to place, space used to be something that could not be reached, because it was outside the experience of place.

Place has often been 'naturalized' – taken for something that is more 'real' than space. When one refers to place, one refers, although not often consciously, to such phenomena as roots, belonging, interpersonal relationships and face-to-face communication. Mattelart (2000: 108) observes that place is triply symbolic because it relates to identity, relationships and history. It symbolizes the relationship of each of its occupants with her/himself, with the other occupants, and with their common history. Obviously, the underlying thought here is that it is something small rather than big, close rather than distant. More often the use of the term 'place' refers to villages, neighbourhoods and communities where people know each other and have interpersonal communication without recourse to media and communications. This is, of course, still how many people live most of their lives: they belong to a community, whether it is their neighbourhood, their workplace or the place they spend their free time. Harvey (1993: 4) refers to the importance of place in the formation of identities, because place is a fundamental means by which people make sense of the world and through which they act. Crang (1998: 102) points out that people do not simply locate themselves, they define themselves through a sense of place. He writes:

> Places provide an anchor of shared experiences between people and continuity over time. Spaces become places as they become 'time-thickened'. They have a past and a future that bind people together round them. The lived connection binds people and places together. It enables people to define themselves and to share experiences with others and form themselves into communities. (1998: 103)

In defining places, one often gets the impression that media and communication are not a part of these. The significance of place is clearly seen in many writers' work, most notably in Heidegger's famous phrase that 'place is the locale of the truth of being'. Heidegger made very few references in his writings to the media, and was disturbed and even terrified at the distancelessness which space–time compression introduced. As Harvey (1993: 14) observes, Heidegger refused to see mediated social relationships with others as in any way expressive of any kind of authenticity. Heidegger is not alone. Many theorists see media and communications as bringing fundamental change to places. For example, Giddens writes:

In pre-modern societies, space and place largely coincide, since the spatial dimensions of social life are, for most of the population, and even in most respects, dominated by 'presence' – by localised activities. The advent of modernity increasingly tears away from place by fostering relations between 'absent' others, locationally distant from any given situation of face-to-face interaction. In conditions of modernity, place becomes increasingly *phantasmagoric*: that is to say, locales are thoroughly penetrated and shaped in terms of social influences quite distant from them. (1990: 18–19)

Although Giddens acknowledges the changing nature of relationships between places, and thus indirectly inside places, he sees places becoming 'phantasmagoric', which could mean 'a shifting series or succession of phantasms or imaginary figures, as seen in a dream or fevered condition, as called up by the imagination, or as created by literary description'.[1] Many time–space theorists see media and communications as things that are unreal and that threaten even the authenticity of places. Relph (1976) makes a distinction between authentic and non-authentic attitudes to places. He writes:

An authentic attitude to place is thus understood to be a direct and genuine experience of the entire complex of the identity of places – not mediated and distorted through a series of quite arbitrary social and intellectual fashions about how the experience should be, nor following stereotyped conventions. It comes from a full awareness of places for what they are as products of man's intentions and the meaningful settings for human activities, or from a profound and unselfconscious identity with place. (1976: 64)

Relph uses the concept of placelessness to describe the lookalike landscapes that result from improved communications, increased mobility and imitation. He points out the role of media and communications in this process by writing that 'mass communication appears to result in a growing uniformity of landscape and a lessening of places by encouraging and transmitting general and standardized tastes and fashions' (1976: 92). According to Relph (1976: 120), among the processes that encourage placelessness are: (1) mass communication and modes of diffusion of mass attitudes and kitsch fashions; and (2) mass culture of dictated and standardized values, maintained by but also making possible mass communication.

Relph's concept of placelessness is not too distant from Augé's (1995) concept of non-place, which is used to describe places like airports, shopping malls and fast food restaurants. Augé distinguishes between 'place' (which is encrusted with historical moments and social life) and 'non-place' (where individuals are connected in a uniform manner and where no organic life is possible). 'Non-places' are like parentheses through which daily life in supermodernity moves. They are defined by words and texts, by tickets, passes, visas and passports (Beynon and Dunkerley, 2000: 35).

Whilst Relph and others have argued that the penetration of media and communication changes places into non-places, Meyrowitz goes one step further in his influential book *No Sense of Place* (1985) where he claims that electronic media affect us not primarily through their content, but by changing the 'situational geography' of social life (1985: 6). He writes:

> Changes in places in the past have always affected the relationship *among* places. They have affected the information that people *bring* to places and the information that people have *in* given places. Electronic media go one step further: they lead to a nearly total dissociation of physical place and 'social' place. When we communicate through telephone, radio, television, or computer, we are physically no longer determined by where and who we are socially. (1985: 115)

When Meyrowitz writes that 'we are physically no longer determined by where and who we are socially' he is referring implicitly to changing identities, where the connection between place and identity has been loosened because of the action of the media and of communications technologies. Meyrowitz concludes that the feeling of 'no sense of place' has increased (1985: 308). Our world is becoming senseless to many because, for the first time in modern history, we are relatively without place: we are part of a global world. Many scholars have referred to this as an identity crisis. Again, before we are able to understand the role of media and communications in this process, we need to tackle the question of space.

SPACE AND THE MEDIA

In contrast to place, space is a much more abstract term; but at the same time it is related to place. Massey writes that 'social relations always have a spatial form and a spatial content . . . Given that it is a construction of space, a place is formed out of the particular set of social relations which interact at a particular location' (1994: 168). De Certeau observes that 'space is a practiced place thus the street geometrically defined by urban planning is transformed into a space by walkers' (1984: 117) is often quoted when people want to understand the difference between place and space. As Lie (2002) observes, in an interpretive sense, this quotation summarizes the difference between space and place. It means that space is a lived place; thus, through (inter)action and communication, places are transformed into spaces and become *spaces of communication*. Further, he writes that:

> places are fixed and stable. Borders of places are set and can precisely be determined. Borders of spaces are flexible and are constructed in a symbolic, interpretative way. Thus, 'walking in the city' transforms the place into space. Moreover, 'watching television in the home' can for instance also be seen as

practiced or lived place. This is not only the case because the home is a geographical defined setting, but also because the television text itself – in De Certeau's words (in the context of a written text) 'a place constituted by a system of signs' (De Certeau, 1984: 117) – is by the act of watching transformed into space. Such, by the act of consumption and interpretation, created *spaces of communication* can be geographical and physical, as well as non-physical and non-geographical.

This is a very different view of the difference between place and space. They are not contradictory, but transitory and as a result often overlapping. Thus the difference between place and space should not be seen in a clear-cut way, where place represents everything that is good and worth protecting threatened by space which seeks to transform it into non-authentic place (space). What we actually see is that place and space are becoming closer to each other, becoming *splace*, largely because of media and communications.

Media and communications transform place and space, not only by connecting places with each other and shortening the distance between them, but by creating new spaces within and outside places where former rules and norms do not necessarily hold. Space could also be seen as something liberating, with elusive boundaries and with new possibilities, but spaces can also become restrictive, closed and hierarchical. Spaces like places are not free of power, and struggles are fought over who is taking control over them.

We have talked about time, place and space in a rather abstract way, almost entirely without the people who live in places, transform places, move from one place to another, discover new places, and combine places with others, thus creating new combinations of places and spaces. All this occurs through time, in time and sometimes on time. While doing all this, people contribute to globalization in which time, place and space are becoming more interrelated because of media and communications.

THREE FAMILIES AND THEIR SENSE OF TIME

So far we have not touched on the experiences of individuals in relation to time, place and space. Most theorists who work on these concepts do not actually research people's experience. To be able to understand what has happened during the last 100 years to individuals in different locations, examples from the three families are used here.

TABLE 3.1 Family 1: time, place and space

	Great-grandmother Tyyne, 1905–87	Grandmother Eila, 1927–	Mother Terhi, 1953–	Son Nyrki, 1976–
Place	Rural village in Juva, industrial town of Kotka	Juva, Kotka, small towns, capital Helsinki, Kotka	Small town of Lappeenranta, Helsinki, global city of London	Helsinki
Home country	Imperial Russia, Finland	Finland, EU citizenship from 1995	Finland, UK, EU citizenship from 1995	Finland, EU citizenship from 1995
Changes in lifestyle	From rural to urban	From rural to urban	From capital to cosmopolitan	Capital
Time	Gregorian and Julian calendars	Gregorian calendar	Gregorian calendar	Gregorian calendar
Media and communication	Books from 1920, newspapers from birth, radio from 1935, magazines from 1938, film from 1936, phone from 1939, television from 1964	Books, newspapers from birth, magazines, radio from early childhood, phone from 1951, television from 1963, video from 1987, computer from 1980 (work), mobile phone from 1994, Internet from 1998	Books, newspapers, magazines, radio, phone from birth, television from 1963, record player from 1967, video from 1987, computer from 1990, Internet from 1990, mobile phone from 1996	Books, newspapers, magazines, radio, television from birth, video, computer from early childhood, mobile phone from 1996

When we look at the history of the first family (Table 3.1), there has also been a significant change in the concept of time. The great-grandmother Tyyne's agrarian way of life in a small farm in Juva was very different from her new life in the industrial community of Sunila in Kotka. Their concept of time in Juva was very much influenced by Tyyne's and her husband Antti's profession as farmers for whom hours were far less important than seasons. In Juva, the family had two clocks: an alarm clock in the bedroom and a wall clock. Only Antti had a personal watch in his pocket. It was a tradition in the countryside that women got a watch (*tissikello*, 'breast watch', in a local dialect), which they wore on a necklace, as their engagement present. Antti could not afford one, and Tyyne got her first personal watch only in the 1940s. Time measured by clocks for them was very much collective time. Only the male in the household had his personal watch, which he did not use daily but was more of a status symbol.

Mechanically measured time did not dictate the family's life, which was much more influenced by their daily responsibilities and the time of day and year. They had to get up early in the morning every morning, no matter what, because the cows had to be milked and fed. The same

FIG 3.1 The new farm in Juva

routine was repeated in the evening. The family's livelihood determined their way of life, not the clocks. There were no entire days off and no holidays. Even on Sunday, on a religious holy day, the cows had to be milked and fed.

Every day was a working day, but Sunday had a special status. On Saturday Tyyne cleaned the house, made porridge in the oven and heated the sauna where everybody went to wash himself or herself in the evening. On Sunday, the family rested and sometimes went to church. Since the church was quite far away from their home, they did not go there every Sunday. They did not have a radio that could bring them broadcast church ceremonies either.

The family followed the Gregorian calendar, with its annual festivities such as Christmas and Easter (religious) in December and April, Midsummer (secular) in June, and Kekri (All Soul's Day, secular, slaughtering of animals, annual pay and holiday for agricultural workers). The calendar also provided for the observance of its followers' own birthdays and name days (marked in the calendar). They had a university calendar hanging next to their kitchen window (the university had an exclusive copyright to publish calendars). There they marked in pencil the days when cows were conceived, seeds were planted, bills were to be paid, and when the meetings of the local farmers' society would be held. They followed closely the waxing and waning of the moon marked on the calendar, since they used this to forecast the weather.

FIG 3.2 Wood transportation in Juva

Since the family had no electricity but oil lamps and candles instead, their days were also influenced by the amount of light. Summers (3 months) were short and light (the 'white nights'), and were followed by rapidly darkening autumns and long dark winters. In the summer, people were able to work long hours (even to cut hay in the middle of the night), but in the winter the days were very short, and it was impossible to grow anything because of the snow. Farmers in Juva, as in many other parts of the country, earned much needed extra money by cutting wood and selling it to the paper mill companies or by working directly for these companies. They worked 6 days a week, thus already starting to follow the timetable of industrial societies. Farmers' wives earned some money by providing board or lodging for the men who came to transport the wood. This was also a time when local people were much more in contact with people from elsewhere.

After Tyyne and Antti lost their farm in the 1930s and had to leave, their life changed drastically. When their agricultural way of life changed to an industrial way of life, this also affected their sense of time. Clocks now became much more important. Tyyne and Antti worked in shifts in order to take care of their children without outside help (which they could not afford even if they had wanted it), and the children had to go to school. It was the factory, the paper mill, that now set their timetable for 6 working days every week. The factory whistle reminded its workers of the beginning and end of each shift. Tyyne and Antti started receiving a weekly salary that was given to them at a certain time on a certain day of the week.

FIG 3.3 Antti (left) building the new paper mill in Sunila, Kotka

They were able to use the laundry and the sauna owned by the paper mill in their neighbourhood, but they could only do this at certain times and often by making a reservation. Many of their previous activities became communal activities, since they met other people doing them. Women did their laundry together, and men and women (separately) took saunas together. Food was bought from shops instead of being produced on their own farm.

Although they worked 6 days a week, their Sunday was now a holiday without work (except household work), when the whole family was at home at the same time. They did not go to church and they were able to

FIG 3.4 The paper mill in Sunila, Kotka

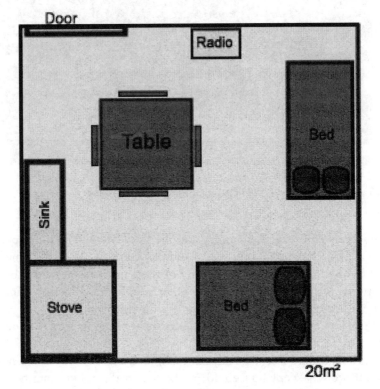

FIG 3.5 Tyyne's and Antti's flat in Sunila, Kotka

sleep longer than on workdays. The family listened to the sermon on the radio on Sunday mornings. Later, they either went to see films at the cinema or, in the winter, skied and skated. The factory had its own clubs for brass bands, sports and choral singing. However, Tyyne and Antti were not active in trade unions or politics, maintaining their agrarian identity and sense of belonging to Juva.

The family had more frequent social contacts in their new location than they had had in Juva, but they were also able to maintain contact with their relatives by writing them letters and later by phoning them. They spent their holidays in Juva, and the children were also sent there when the war broke out and Kotka was bombed. In this way, with their 'big leap' from the agrarian to the industrial way of life, their social relations became stretched in the Giddensian manner. Their regular social contacts did not extend beyond these places, but they became more aware of other places, because a new space, an independent nation-state called Finland, had been created in 1917.

The creation of a nation-state also had an effect on their sense of time, because new nations start to celebrate not only religious but also national holidays. Finns had followed the Gregorian calendar even before 1917, when they were subjects of Imperial Russia, which at that time used the Julian calendar. The Gregorian calendar remained official even after independence, but some use was made of the Julian calendar. A new sense of common history was created, and Independence Day marked the

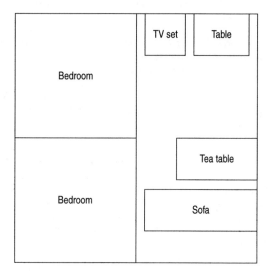

FIG 3.6 Qinghe's and Ju Hua's house in Dong Xiao Wu

beginning of that era. The national broadcasting company that was established in 1927 also increased the collective sense of experience of time through its regular broadcasting of events such as news and sports that reminded the new citizens of their belongingness.

The experience of time by the early members of family 1 was not very different from the two oldest generations of family 2 (Table 3.2). They stayed in place for much longer, and only the youngest generation left the village. However, the way of life of the villagers changed from agrarian to semi-agrarian when the brick factory was established in the village in 1974. The collectivization of agriculture also brought changes into the villages, when villagers started to work more together and were being paid for their work.

TABLE 3.2 Family 2: time, place and space

	Great-grandfather Baosheng, 1888–1971	Grandfather Zhansheng, 1923–2000	Father Qinghe, 1944–	Son Junjie, 1974–
Place	Dong Xiao Wu village	Dong Xiao Wu village	Dong Xiao Wu village and Ci County	Dong Xiao Wu village, Ci County, Beijing, London, Los Angeles
Home country	China under Qing Dynasty until 1912, Republic of China 1912–49, Japanese occupation 1937–45, People's Republic of China 1949–	Republic of China 1912–49, Japanese occupation 1937–45, People's Republic of China 1949–	Republic of China 1912–49, Japanese occupation 1937–45, People's Republic of China 1949–	People's Republic of China 1949–
Changes in lifestyle	From feudalism to socialism	More diversified rural life than previous generation	From rural to urban	From rural to capital and to cosmopolitan
Time	First only Chinese, later Gregorian and Chinese calendars	Gregorian and Chinese calendars	Gregorian and Chinese calendars	Gregorian and Chinese calendars
Media and communication	Government loudspeaker installed at home in people's commune in the 1960s, books from 1900s, film from 1950s, radio from 1960s	Books from 1930s, newspaper seldom, radio from 1960s often, magazines seldom, film from 1950s, telephone from 1990s, computer never	Books from 1940s, newspapers 1950s, radio 1960s, magazines 1950s, film 1950s, phone 1980s, television 1970s, computer and Internet sometimes	Books 1970s, newspapers 1980s, radio 1980s, magazines 1980s, film 1980s, television 1980s (first private TV set in 1985), computer and Internet 1990s

Compared with the first family, the second family stayed in place for three generations, but we still see a change in their use of media and communication. Unlike the first family, which had wider access to media and communication only when they moved to town, the second family gained wider access in their own village because of the loudspeakers that the government installed there. It was a more collective experience than that of the Finnish family: people listened to the radio or watched television collectively outdoors instead of indoors at home. But the media were there to remind them regularly and repeatedly that they now belonged to a larger community, to a nation, that they had a national belongingness, although much later than for the first family.

At the time when family 1 was still living in Juva and family 2 was living in Dong Xiao Wu, Moshe, the great-grandfather of family 3, was already living in Zilupe, a small town. All the connections that the first two families lacked were already available for the third family in their urban way of life at the beginning of the twentieth century: telephone, regular newspapers and even a record player (Table 3.3). Still, Moshe strictly observed his religious calendar, which was not the calendar used by the majority of people in his town.

The urban environment was not enough for Moshe's son Lasik, who started planning his emigration to a new place in a new country and

FIG 3.7 Dong Xiao Wu village

TABLE 3.3 Family 3

	Great-grandfather Moshe, 1881–1941	Grandfather Lasik, 1912–97	Father Nechemya, 1941–	Daughter Shani, 1972–
Place	Small town Zilupe (20,000 people)	Zilupe, kibbutz (rural) in Kinneret	Kibbutz, cities around the world, back to towns in Israel	Kibbutz, cities abroad, back to Israel, then to London
Home country	Latvia	Latvia, Palestine, Israel	Palestine, Israel	Israel
Changes in lifestyle	No changes	From urban diasporic lifestyle to collective lifestyle of kibbutz (rural)	From collective lifestyle (rural) to private urban lifestyle	From collective lifestyle (rural) to urban lifestyle, from local to international/ global
Time	Hebrew and Julian calendars	First Julian and then Hebrew calendars	Hebrew and Gregorian calendars when abroad	Gregorian and Hebrew calendars
Media and communication	Books (Russian and Yiddish), religious books, daily newspaper in Yiddish, gramophone, telephone (only for business matters, located in the shop)	Books, newspapers, radio, cinema, television (since age 55), public phone (since age 42), domestic phone (since age 63)	Books, newspapers, radio, cinema, public phone (since age 18), VCR (since age 29), computer and Internet (since age 54), mobile phone (since age 59)	Books, newspapers, radio, cinema, television, VCR (since age 10), computer (since age 20), Internet (since age 23), mobile phone (since age 25)

getting information about the possibilities. Lasik's new place, the kibbutz in Kinneret, was of course much more isolated than his former home town. It was primarily a farming community that was more inward than outward looking in its attitude, with its socialist Zionist mission. However, of the three families, it was this family that started to live a life not only in two places like our first family but also in two different countries, long before the others. After Lasik left, he kept in contact with his relatives back home by writing letters. These were not frequent and they took a long time to arrive. Their contacts between places were not electronic or instant, but nevertheless contributed to the sense of globalization: an increasing awareness of many places in different countries instead of one country.

FIG 3.8 Laundresses at the summer camp in Zilupe

In all these families the introduction of a new national space brought changes in their sense of time and nationalized their sense of time: in their respective countries they more or less follow the same calendars with national and religious holidays. In this way, their place and their national space are used to define their sense of time. This is not fully the case any longer. Shani, Junjie, Terhi, the members of the three families who left their home countries, live simultaneously according to the calendar and the time of their present and past locations.

Shani observes some of the Jewish holidays, although not all, with her friends and relatives in London. She is able to buy the ingredients needed for special dishes in Finchley, a Jewish neighbourhood in London. Junjie also observed major Chinese holidays, such as New Year, in London, but lived his daily life according to the local calendar and time. Unlike Shani, who only shops for food for major Jewish and Israeli holidays, Junjie insisted on eating Chinese food every day.

Terhi's Finnish calendar is very similar to the British one, because they are both based on the Protestant religion. For the first time in her life she experienced that Christmas Eve is not necessarily the major day of celebration outside Finland; British people still work, shop and cook when her fellow Finns have already gone home to celebrate. She also misses Vappu (First of May), a traditional day of celebration for workers and students, and Juhannus (Midsummer), originally an ancient pagan festivity of light and fertility, which marks the summer solstice, neither of which are celebrated in the UK. Her relatives and friends who visit her bring rye bread, gravad lax (marinated salmon), Emmenthal cheese and salmiakki (a salty black liquorice-like sweet), or she can buy these at a Finnish church in London.

However, by and large, Shani, Junjie and Terhi all primarily live the local life, though combined with elements of the calendar they used when they were still living in their home countries. They are more aware of different times, they can cross time zones with technology, they can combine different calendars, and they can also pick and choose the elements they want to include in their lives. For them, things have never been as dramatic as they were for Shani's grandfather Lasik, who left and never went back.

Time is still a factor in the daily lives of each of those family members who live in their home country. Each family follows local time and lives its daily life accordingly. However, the families live in different time zones: while Finland and Israel are on the same time, China is 6 hours ahead. From London, Helsinki and Tel Aviv are 2 hours ahead and Beijing is 8 hours ahead. Whenever Terhi, Junjie and Shani want to call their family members, they need to think about the time. With their global experience, when one family member lives abroad they all start taking into account the local time in another country.

Electronic media and communications, whether the telephone or the Internet, cross time zones without the effort of travel and without taking into account the time of day in the country of arrival. It is up to the receiver whether she/he picks up the phone or opens her/his computer mail. Harvey's notion of the unimportance of spatial distance is well exemplified in the use of media and communications, but that use still needs to be thought of in terms of time distance. The lives of all families, independent of their members' location, are determined by the difference between day and night and are thus lived in accordance with local time. Mediated globalization has resulted in an increasing sense of time. Having said this, when Terhi, living in London, after giving careful consideration to the 2 hours' time difference, tries to call her son at 12 noon Finnish time and wakes him up, she thinks that young people have their own universal time zone that is independent of any existing time zones!

THREE FAMILIES' SENSE OF PLACE

For all the families in question, place has mattered a lot and still does, and a loss of place is common to all of them. Shani's grandfather Lasik's loss of place (and of language) when he left his home country for another was

FIG 3.9 Lasik (left) with his fellow kibbutzniks building a 'Homa Umigdal' in a new kibbutz

FIG 3.10 Kibbutz children (Nechemya in the middle) in the children's house in Kinneret

never forgotten. Nyrki's great-grandparents Tyyne's and Antti's loss of the farm in Juva was probably the most significant event for them. Nyrki's mother Terhi's move to London also meant a significant change in her lifestyle and social contacts and a change of language. She, like Shani and Junjie, experiences homesickness periodically. They all miss places, which they now occasionally dream about, and these places have become to a certain extent phantasmagoric. Everything, in their minds, is as it was when *they* left the place. The longer they stay away, the more imaginary the picture of the place becomes.

They all find that life in London is very hectic compared to life in their countries of origin. London is a global city, and global cities live in their own time. Terhi's mother Eila bought back a summer cottage her parents built in 1945 to give their family a flavour of the agricultural life they missed in a flat in Kotka. Life at the cottage, although ironically now a part of Kotka city, imitates the agrarian way of life where generation after generation do things as they have always been done without most modern facilities. The family goes back centuries to partially produce its own food and cook it in primitive conditions. Eila lives there for 3 months of every year; Terhi goes there for her summer holiday with her husband; and even Nyrki, who like Terhi used to think that the life there was boring, has now started going there. Time stops at the cottage: it has a radio and the smallest possible black and white television. Life is again mainly controlled by the sun and activities that are repeated every day, such as heating the sauna, taking a sauna and eating supper after the sauna.

Terhi even finds going to Helsinki relaxing, because it is still a relatively small city (500,000 inhabitants) without the problems of London. Shani also commented after her last holiday in Tel Aviv (2.5 million inhabitants), one of the biggest cities in Israel, how relaxing her time there was because of the pace of life. Junjie thinks the big change for him was the move from his home village to Beijing. Beijing (almost 14 million inhabitants) and London (7 million inhabitants) are in the same league, compared with his village. Interestingly, global capitals, whatever their location, offer their inhabitants an experience that can be transferred to another global capital. This partly explains why Shani and Junjie feel so comfortable in London. They also allow their inhabitants to have elements in their daily life from their countries of origin because these cultures are present in the global cities.

Media and communications again play a significant part in this experience. Shani calls her mother every single day, Terhi her mother and children every week, and Junjie his mother once every 2 weeks. The cost of telephone calls partly explains the difference in frequency; partly it is also a gender issue. Shani, Terhi and Junjie also have access to news, films, music and literature from their respective countries. London is one of the most connected cities in the world and this is reflected in the daily lives of its inhabitants.

THREE FAMILIES AND THEIR SENSE OF SPACE

What unites all three families is the creation of new national space; each of them has experienced this, whatever their location. In the formation of national space, time and place are also present. The essential requirement for a successful project is the construction of a new 'community' that connects one's location with other locations and thus creates new space.

As Zerubavel (2003: 13) shows, time plays an important role in the construction of *mnemonic communities*. According to him, one of the most remarkable features of human memory is the ability to mentally transform an essentially unstructured series of events into seemingly coherent *historical narratives*. They are often timed to start with the date and year to celebrate independence. According to Zerubavel (2003: 46–7), an annual cycle of commemorative holidays is one of the main functions of the calendar in helping to ensure that people periodically revisit their collective past and also to socialize them in their mnemonic community. For example, the Finnish calendar marks 6 December to celebrate Finnish Independence Day (1917); in the Israeli calendar Independence Day is celebrated annually on 5 Iyar, on the anniversary of the establishment of the state of Israel (14 May 1948); and the Chinese calendar marks 1 October to celebrate the founding of the Republic in 1949. These dates also mark historical discontinuity, historical cutting, to differentiate one period from the next (2003: 82).

All three families have experienced an increasing sense of belonging from a place to a space. They first lived and experienced their life locally, but then developed a sense of belonging to a bigger community, a nation. In this process, media and communications have played a significant role. As Anderson (1983) has noted, all the citizens of one country are never able to meet each other, but they share a sense of belonging mainly through the media. The media keeps *flagging* (Billig, 1995: 8) them about their citizenship, their mnemonic community, their nation. First it was the daily newspaper that served this function, later national broadcasting companies.

The timing of the establishment of nationhood is different for each of the families, and accordingly the establishment of national media. The National Broadcasting Company, Yleisradio (General Broadcaster) was founded in 1926 in Finland. Transmissions were made first from the Home Guard radio station, and later from the Army Signal Battalion station, both in Helsinki.[2]

Radio was first installed in Israel after the founding of the state, in the Prime Minister's office, to act in the service of the government. Only in 1965 did Israeli radio become a public authority. Television also came late to Israel compared with other countries because of opposition to it, mainly for religious reasons. The Israeli government originally conceived the establishment of television as a bridge to the Arab population in the occupied territories, which had been exposed only to broadcasts from Arab countries after the Six Day War in 1967.[3]

The Chinese Communist Party established its first radio station in December 1940 and started transmitting in a temple about 19 miles from Yan'an, the revolutionary base of the Communists in north-west China. The station was part of an all-out offensive strategy against the Nationalist government in the country. The programmes were intended for audiences in the territories occupied by the Nationalist government, and they disseminated news and commentaries about the 'liberated' areas and policies of the Chinese Communist Party (Chang, 1989: 185; Lull, 1991: 19–20). After the Communists came to power in 1949 they took over 49 radio stations operated by the Nationalist government and established 17 new ones. However, there were only one million radio sets, mainly in industrial areas and big cities. To facilitate broadcasting in rural areas, loudspeakers were installed for collective listening in the countryside (Chang, 1989: 34).

All our families started to live in nation-states founded between 1917 and 1949. These new political spaces were constructed and maintained, in part at least, by national media. The new political space gradually affected their sense of place extending it into an identification with a national space.

CONCLUSION

By combining globalization theories with the everyday practice of the three families, we can see where these theories work and where they do not. As Massey (1994: 152–64) has observed, social relations, which are the essence of social space, are decreasingly place-bound or contained in the boundaries of a physical locale. One issue has been whether social relations become more distant or more intense because of time–space distanciation or compression.

In the lives of the three families we have seen both effects: some contacts have become more intense, while others have become more distant. Globalization as such does not necessarily have anything to do with this outcome. The Finnish great-grandparents' move from Juva to Kotka resulted in a drift in their granddaughter Terhi's life. She no longer experiences intense and frequent contact with her relatives in Juva: most of them she has never met, and knows only by name because her mother and grandmother talked about them. Shani knows very little about her family history in Latvia and does not identify herself as somebody who came from Latvia. Partly this has happened because most of her family members were killed during World War II and the memories are simply too painful; partly it is because she now has a new and much more distinct national identity that is based on similarity rather than differences. Even Junjie, whose family has stayed in place, knows very little about his great-grandparents' lives. Memory in families seldom reaches further than two generations back. It is possible to reach further and further horizontally across space, but seldom vertically across past time. Memory across time depends on what Williams (1980: 64–6) described as the *structure of feeling*, which disappears with the dead.

The fact that all these families live in different time zones also has an effect on their daily lives. We can clearly see how more frequent connections between the different family members make them more aware of the differences not only in their use of time but also in their sense of time. It is a matter not merely of different times zones, but also of the pace of time, of how time is experienced. Those members of the families who live abroad – Shani, Junjie and Terhi – miss their experience of time in their home countries, but can also go back to experience it. Those members of the families who are still in place, but live in urban centres, also want to go back to experience agrarian time. This is why three generations of a Finnish family go back to spend time in a summer cottage built by the first generation.

According to many theorists, the sense of place has been fundamentally changed by the arrival of media and communications. Their presence changes places into spaces. One can easily understand that there are new placeless spaces, such as airports or shopping malls, but even there social relationships are formed between people which could make them places. There is a real danger of falling for the Heideggerian picture of the unspoilt original village that is lost forever with modernization and/or globalization.

Places do change. Juva, where the Finnish great-grandmother once lived, is still today a living small community of more than 7000 inhabitants, with its own schools, libraries, health centre, and industry. It has lost half of its population because of emigration to big cities. Only 20 per cent of its remaining inhabitants still earn their living from farming. The most important industries are carpentry and printing.[4]

Junjie's village has lost many of its collective features compared with the old people's commune. There are no remains of the collective dining rooms of the old commune, which were free and popular in the village. The cooks are still often invited to cook food for weddings and funerals. Nominal political socialism and economic capitalism both exist in the village, but most people have left the village to find a better life elsewhere. The land still belongs to the state, but more and more people prefer to have it privatized.

Collective and anti-consumerist ideologies are still strong among old people who hold on to their positive memories from Chairman Mao's era. Young people have adopted the consumerist ideology promoted by electronic media. In Junjie's village today 98 per cent of the 523 families (2183 people) have at least one television set. The total number of television sets is around 530. The number of telephones in the village was 92 in August 2002 (Song, 2003).

Shani's kibbutz has changed significantly, but is still a kibbutz, unlike many others. However, it has gone through significant changes following a process of privatization, like most of the kibbutzim in Israel. The kibbutz members are now earning differential salaries according to their contribution to the kibbutz's profit; meals are now sold in the communal dining room (they used to be free), and only one meal a day is now served (it used to be open all day, serving three meals). By and large, the kibbutz operates more like a communal settlement; most people still know each other, but there are fewer communal spaces and activities than there used to be, and the capitalist system is rapidly taking over socialist idealism.

Media and communications have contributed to connectivity in a way that not even travel has been able to do. Many people remain in their place, as do Junjie's family members. What many theorists of place have failed to acknowledge is the increasing connectivity, not only between global places, but also within places. Whether it is Juva, Kotka, Dong Xiao Wu or Kinneret, not only are places more connected with the outside, wider world, but also interconnectivity has increased both within the place and with other places. Does this give these places a quality of 'placelessness'? Have they become lookalikes that are less authentic, more phantasmagoric? Do Juva, Dong Xiao Wu and Kinneret now look more similar to each other? Have they become placeless because of the presence of media and communications?

I do not think so. These places are distinctively different from each other, owing to such factors as language, natural environment, climate, traditions, people and so on. The thing that has changed is that they are connected both internally and externally. They have become space because of those connections, but they are definitely not placeless. If those connections did not exist, they would be left out of that space. However, the consequences of increasing connectivity and even further mediation have not yet been discussed. This will be the topic of the next three chapters.

NOTES

1 http://athens.oed.com/, 14 August 2003.
2 http://www.oldradio.com/archives/international/finland.html, 8 August 2003.
3 htttp://www.museum.tv/archives, 15 June 2003.
4 www.juva.fi, 7 August 2003.

4 HOMOGENIZATION

One cannot study the consequences of globalization without acknowledging that the outcome can be either homogenization or heterogenization, or even both, depending on specific circumstances. We simply do not yet know enough about the complex nature of globalization where connectivity has become increasingly mediated. As shown in Chapter 1, before the advent of the globalization debate it was the field of international communication which was dealing, in media and communications studies, with issues of globalization, although the term was not being used.

Sreberny (1996: 178–9) has distinguished three models in the field of international communication: (1) communications and development; (2) cultural imperialism; and (3) cultural pluralism. In each of these models, the introduction of media and communications has had different consequences. The communications and development paradigm emerged in the early 1960s when the promotion of the use of media and communications especially in the developing countries was seen to alter attitudes and values. This was a period when their role was discovered and they were seen as powerful agents for change. The cultural imperialism model argued that far from helping these countries to develop, the international flows of technology transfer and media 'hardware' coupled with the 'software' flows of cultural products actually strengthened the one-way dependency between developed and developing countries and prevented true development. Again, media and communications were seen as powerful, possibly even more powerful than in the previous paradigm since they could threaten the cultural independence of these nations. The third model, the cultural pluralism paradigm, criticized the earlier models as being based on a situation of comparative global media scarcity, limited global players and embryonic media systems in developing countries. The 'global pluralists' adopt an optimistic voice regarding the diversity of media producers and locales and the many loops of cultural flows that have merged.

Although Sreberny refers not to paradigms but to models, it is possible to see these transitions as paradigm changes in the Kuhnian (1962) sense. The different paradigms of international communication are no different from other paradigm changes. From unwavering optimism about the power of media technology in modernizing societies, the paradigm shifted to complete pessimism about its negative influences. In the final stage, pessimism again gave way to optimism, when the audience was seen to have its own power. In each of these shifts, what existed before has been replaced with something new, often moving from one extreme to another.

Looking back, it is of course easy to see that it is not the introduction of media technology as such which changes societies; rather, there is a much more complex process which cannot be reduced to a single factor. Again, to see global media companies as all-powerful evil empires which only harm national cultures is no less of an exaggeration in the opposite direction. And finally, to endow the audience with as much power as the media corporations again shows how drastic is the difference between one paradigm and another.

Each of these paradigms views the consequences of the globalization of media differently, but broadly as a process of either homogenization or heterogenization. Even scholars outside the media and communication studies field are now aware of the homogenization/heterogenization debate, which has not only dominated media and communication studies for several decades, but contributed to its division into media and cultural studies. As Short and Kim observe:

> The debates on cultural globalization have polarized into whether the recent surge of cultural flows and global consciousness has increased or decreased sameness between places around the world. The tension between cultural homogenization and cultural heterogenization is the most controversial issue in the interpretation of increasing actions in the world. (1999: 75)

However, what has been absent in this debate is the question: what is homogeneous and what is heterogeneous? Before answering that, a distinction has to be made between culture and media, although this is not always clear. Boyd-Barrett (1977: 118–19) has observed that the media are possibly the most influential single component of cultural imperialism. Following this line of argumentation, media either homogenize or heterogenize cultures (Table 4.1). The assumption in the imperialism paradigm was that the global media were homogenizing, while in the cultural pluralism paradigm the *local* media come to be seen as heterogenizing. But where does that leave the national media?

The question of whether the national media are homogenizing or heterogenizing has been largely ignored in all of these paradigms. The idea that national media can be just as homogenizing as global media opens up a new way of thinking about homogenization and heterogenization. In the cultural imperialism paradigm the national was celebrated as something worth protecting, without taking into account that it could be as oppressive to many people as the global.

The homogenization/heterogenization issue has clearly been the main contribution of media and cultural studies to the globalization debate. This debate started even before the globalization debate, so media scholars were already engaged in debating the consequences of globalization before they

TABLE 4.1 Different paradigms of the global, the national and the local

Paradigm	Global media seen as?	National media seen as?	Local media seen as?	Consequences
Communications and development	Homogeneous	Homogeneous	?	Homogeneous
Cultural imperialism	Homogeneous	Homogeneous	Homogeneous	Homogeneous
Cultural pluralism	Heterogeneous	?	Heterogeneous	Heterogeneous

began to discuss whether globalization existed and what was the role in globalization of media and communications. The pioneering role of media scholars in acknowledging the power of the global media should not be underestimated, but they did not contribute much to the main debate on globalization. Some media theorists defined globalization (and some still do) solely in terms of media/cultural imperialism.

The terminology needs further attention here. Boyd-Barrett, in defining media imperialism, wrote that 'it refers to a much more specific range of phenomena than the term "cultural imperialism" . . . It is also possibly the single most important component of cultural imperialism outside formal educational institutions, from the viewpoint of those who are actively engaged in extending or containing given cultural influences' (1977: 119). It is interesting that proponents of the cultural imperialism theory saw the media as the single most important component in cultural imperialism, but that this has not been the case in the globalization debate. The importance of media and communications has been acknowledged in the sphere of cultural globalization, but not in definitions of globalization. The early media imperialism theorists, although only discussing cultural imperialism, were right in pointing out the important role of the media.

Cultural imperialism theories were mainly associated with the USA. This is not surprising since many of the early proponents of cultural imperialism were in Latin America where US influence was probably more visible than anywhere else. As Roach (1997: 47) has observed, the concept of cultural imperialism was most prominent in Latin America (see, for example, Pasquali, 1963; Beltrán, 1976; Kaplún, 1973; Reyes Matta, 1977), but was also put forward by such scholars as Smythe (1981), Schiller (1976), Boyd-Barrett (1977), and Mattelart (1979).

Schiller defined the concept of cultural imperialism as:

the sum of the processes by which a society is brought into the modern world system and how its dominating stratum is *attracted, pressured, forced, and sometimes bribed* into shaping social institutions to correspond to, or even promote, the value and structures of the dominating centre of the system. (1976: 9)

For Schiller, the unit of analysis was a society belonging to a world system in which different societies had unequal power and were thus divided into core and peripheral countries. Schiller's definition was very much a child of its time – international relations and international communication being the parents.

Boyd-Barrett defines media imperialism in action when

> the country which originates an international media influence either *exports* this influence as a deliberate political strategy, or simply *disseminates* this influence unintentionally or without deliberation in a more general process of political, social or economic influence. The country which is affected by media influence either *adopts* this influence as a deliberate commercial or political strategy, or simply *absorbs* this influence unreflectively as the result of the contract. (1977: 119)

Boyd-Barrett's unit of analysis is a country, but he actually explicitly refers to the international media of the country that either exports or disseminates influence. Neither Schiller nor Boyd-Barrett mentions individuals or their experiences in these countries. For Boyd-Barrett, media imperialism is 'the process whereby the ownership, structure, distribution or content of media in any one country are singly or together subject to substantial external pressures from media interests of any other country or countries without proportionate reciprocation of influence by the country so affected' (1977: 117). The units of analysis for Boyd-Barrett are the ownership, structure, distribution or media content of individual countries.

There are several similarities between Schiller's and Boyd-Barrett's definitions. The starting point in both of them is that this is a relationship in which the influence originates either in a dominant centre of the world system or in another country. Secondly, although Boyd-Barrett admits the unintentional character of this influence, both he and Schiller acknowledge that a society or country can only adapt or adjust under pressure, or be forced or bribed. Interestingly, Schiller also refers to attraction, thus indicating that a dominant centre is also a pole of attraction.

The cultural/media imperialism concept has a number of merits. First, it is a macro-level analysis based on a political and economic analysis of a world system. Secondly, it acknowledges the uneven character of this process by pointing out the scarcity of resources in some societies and countries compared with others. Schiller and Boyd-Barrett both refer explicitly to the role of the United States in this process. Thirdly, it acknowledges that as a result of this uneven relationship, there is an effect on less developed cultures and societies.

The last point is the most contested. It sounds plausible as long as we are talking in general terms, but when we start asking what kind of consequences we are looking at, it is much more difficult to formulate a solid, empirically tested argument. As several authors have noted, this is the weakest link in the concept. As Golding and Harris write with reference to the concept of media imperialism:

> Firstly it overstates external determinants and undervalues the internal dynamics, not least those of resistance, within dependent societies. Secondly, it conflates economic power and cultural effects. Thirdly, there is an assumption that audiences are passive, and that local and oppositional creativity is of little significance. Finally, there is an often patronizing assumption that what is at risk is the 'authentic' and organic culture of the developing world under the onslaught of something synthetic and inauthentic coming from the West. (1997: 5)

However, Schiller's and Boyd-Barrett's definitions never mention people, who are simply not explicitly included in their definitions. We can, of course, argue that they do implicitly include people because they expect people living in a society or country to manifest a uniform response to this influence. Even theorists who do not talk in terms of countries or societies do talk in terms of cultures, but again without explicit reference to people. For example, when Tunstall (1977: 57) writes that local cultures are being battered out of existence by Western (mainly American) media products, he does not include people. Tunstall also referred explicitly to mainly American media products. As the title of his book *The Media are American* indicated, cultural and media imperialism became identified primarily with the United States. The book's subtitle *Anglo-American Media in the World* (1977) and his later book *The Anglo-American Media Connection* (Tunstall and Machin, 1999) also acknowledged the UK as a source of global media influence.

A CRITIQUE OF MEDIA IMPERIALISM

The faults of media imperialism theory are many and have been pointed out on a number of occasions. In the 1980s and 1990s, media and cultural imperialism theories became a target for criticism by many media and cultural studies scholars, most notably Boyd-Barrett (1982), McQuail (1994), Schlesinger (1991), Tomlinson (1991) and Golding and Harris (1997). Most of the criticism was influenced by audience studies and cultural studies, both of which gave attention to the independent role of culture. This is clearly something which media/cultural imperialism theorists had missed, and the criticism has been largely approved.

One of the most comprehensive critiques has been that of Boyd-Barrett (1998), one of the authors of the original concept. He admits that the original media imperialism thesis was wrong in several respects:

1. It assumed that nation-states are the basic building blocks within the field of global media activities, and that there is a simple association between particular media and particular countries. In fact media

systems are often complex hybrids of different agencies and actors, and thus it is not advisable to make a simple identification of whole corporations with particular national identities. This is precisely why we need to take account of the multi-dimensionality of media activity.

2   It further assumed that it is in the interests of one country to reject or oppose media imperialism on the part of another country in the name of national interest. However, there is often no single national interest but separate media enterprises, which compete against each other both nationally and globally.

3   It did not consider the strategic social structural position of the individuals and interest groups who benefited from facilitating US market entry or even from taking their own initiatives.

4   It did not take into account the question of the audience, but concentrated solely on the production process.

5   It tended to identify the USA as the single centre of a process of media-centric capitalist influence, which flowed outward to the rest of the world in the form of television programmes.

6   It assumed that these programmes had an inevitable and self-sufficient ideological effect upon their helpless audiences on the periphery.

7   It considered experience of media to be beyond the scope of research, or to be simply a homogeneous phenomenon.

McGuigan scarcely exaggerates in calling media imperialism 'deeply unfashionable and problematic' (1992: 229) in the late 1980s and early 1990s. This may be true, but there are still reasons why the concept of cultural imperialism, and within it of media imperialism, has to be taken seriously. As Tomlinson (1997: 175) observes, this is first because certain assumptions of cultural imperialism continue to find a voice in the work of some major, and sophisticated, cultural critics (Hall, 1991; Said, 1993). Secondly, real cultural policy issues demonstrate how seriously some national governments continue to take the threat of cultural imperialism. And thirdly, there are issues posed within this perspective which command the attention of anyone viewing the globalization process with a critical eye (Tomlinson, 1997: 175).

There is also a further reason why the concept of homogenization has to be taken seriously. I would rather use the term 'homogenization' than 'cultural/media imperialism' since both the global and the national can be seen as processes of homogenization. So far, the influence perceived as coming from outside has been seen as homogenization. However, whilst this has been acknowledged, what has not been acknowledged is that, because the global has been seen as homogeneous, the nature of the national has not been questioned. In the same way as the global can be seen as either homogenizing or heterogenizing, so can the national. Somehow the impact of the national as a homogenizing factor has been ignored in this analysis. The media imperialism school also romanticized the national, instead of seeing it as potentially as oppressive as the global.

One of the challenges in multi-local analysis is to see both the global and the national in the everyday life of individuals. If we acknowledge the role of media and communications in globalization we need also to acknowledge that the outcome of this marriage can be either homogenization or heterogenization or both, depending on the historical situation and circumstances. In a multi-sited analysis, the challenge is to be able to see how people are connected to each other not only in their reception but also in their use of media and communications. As a result of this mediated connectivity, they may be influenced by homogeneous media in their localities. However, this homogenization is not caused only by globalization; it can also be caused by nationalism. Furthermore, its possible consequences can be seen not only in the access, content or structures of the media, but also in the larger context of time and space.

EARLY INFLUENCES

Some media homogenization scholars extend the concept of influence even into such developed countries as Finland. Kivikuru (1988: 85) has described Finland as a small Western post-industrial periphery where mass communication dependence adopts a sophisticated form, but is none-theless present. Its structure and volume are not vastly different from those in a situation of equality, but the physical and operational infra-structure reveals dependence on more developed countries. Kivikuru analyses the growth of Anglo-American influence on Finnish media since World War II, concentrating mainly on new media and entertainment.

This type of macro-approach is important, as we saw in Chapter 2 where Robertson's and Innis's periodizations were introduced. Innis refers to different monopolies, which dominated each of the periods, but he never includes the present period in his analysis. Neither does McLuhan, or any of the globalization theorists who defined globalization as an individual experience, pay attention to the unequal power of the media. When the individual members of our three families in Chapter 2 were influenced by the various scapes, they also experienced different periods of domination within them. While most cultural/media imperialism theorists have concentrated on the Anglo-American period, theorists such as Innis have reminded us of the ancient empires such as Rome and of their power. However, if we define globalization as beginning with the first electronic media of the nineteenth century, the Anglo-American period remains the most long-standing and influential period to date, at least in some countries, but not necessarily in every country. This is why it is important to study countries like China or any country where Western influence is a relatively recent phenomenon.

If we look at the first family, we can see how short the Anglo-American period is. Of course, the origin of news or entertainment was not their primary concern. In Juva, Tyyne and Antti read their newspapers when they had time or access to them, but probably did not pay much attention to the sources of foreign news. News became more important to them when Tyyne's sister started to plan her emigration to the USA in the 1920s and needed to know more about the country. It is important to note, as we did in Chapter 3, that in the twentieth century these people had already acquired through the news an increasing sense of place (Rantanen,

FIG 4.1 Antti as a soldier with his daughters Eila and Sisko in Kotka

FIG 4.2 Terhi with a Finnish flag in Kotka

2003). The world started to become more reachable than ever before because of time–space compression.

The very same thing happened to the third family's grandfather Lasik, who was also reading his newspaper in his home town of Zilupe and who started dreaming of emigration to a country that he dreamt would become his. He also received his news from newspapers, but probably had alternative sources through his local Zionist organization. The great-grandfather of the second family, Baosheng, did not have any access to the media before the 1950s, when the Chinese government installed loudspeakers in people's homes to broadcast political propaganda and the music of Chinese opera.

The first generations of both Chinese and Finnish families lived in small, relatively isolated communities where they had either no access (Chinese) or relatively little access (Finnish) to media and communications. Although the Finnish family was poor, they were able to subscribe to and read a regional paper that came out three times a week. The Latvian great-grandfather Moshe, by contrast, was already an urban man and had not only access to urban media (film, telephone) but the means to purchase private media (gramophone).

It would be too easy to conclude that class or economics are the only things that matter, but certainly they both have an influence. Finland and China were both considered poor countries in the early twentieth century, but literacy and media availability account for a difference between the two families. When one compares these two families to the family in Latvia, one can easily see that wealth and an urban lifestyle also mean increasing access to media and communications. The combination of class difference (in this case between peasantry and petty bourgeoisie), literacy and urban lifestyle made and still make a considerable difference and opened access to the wider world beyond national boundaries if one wished.

NATIONAL IDENTITY AND THE MEDIA

Globalization challenges the traditional ways of thinking about nationalism, which are based on the idea that people who live in a given geographical territory share a *national identity*, that they *feel* they *belong* to the same nation. This is often done by underlining the differences between different nations, especially neighbour nations (Hall, 1991: 21–2). Citizens are assumed to share one national identity even if they do not know their fellow citizens and differ from them in multiple ways. Despite the obvious fact that nationalism is as much about exclusion as it is about inclusion (Schlesinger, 1987: 235), it has been the most successful ideology around the world for the last two centuries. By its nature it is a homogeneous ideology, because it is often constructed on an idea of a historically unbroken cord between one nation, one people, one religion, one language, one identity. In reality this had never been the case for obvious reasons, and nationalism increasingly has to include differences but still hold to the idea of sharedness. National identity is also only one of several identities, albeit traditionally considered the most important one (Larrain, 1994: 143). As a result, it is often in conflict with people's other identities, for example their religious or ethnic or political identity.

However, as Anderson (1983: 15–16) wrote in his seminal work, the nation is always imagined because the members of even the smallest nation will never know most of their fellow members, meet them, or even hear of them, yet in the minds of each live the images of their communion. The simple scale of any national space and the shortness of collective memory (Smith, 1990: 179) need the media to construct and maintain the sense of continuity and common destiny among supposed fellow citizens. Anderson referred to the role of printed communication, books and particularly the press in this process, and media scholars (Scannell, 1989; Price, 1995) have further pointed to the role of electronic media, especially broadcasting. Since nationalism has to be kept alive by reminding the members of the nation of their belongingness (Billig, 1995), it is a never-ending process. Hall writes:

FIG 4.3 Junjie (second from right) with his fellow students at Tienanmen Square, Beijing

It is not something that already exists, transcending place, time, history and culture. Cultural identities come from somewhere, have histories. But like everything which is historical, they undergo constant transformation. Far from being eternally fixed in some essential past, they are subject to the continuous 'play' of history, culture and power. Far from being grounded in a mere 'recovery' of the past, which is waiting to be found, and which when found will secure our sense of ourselves into eternity, identities are the names we give to the different ways we are positioned by, and position ourselves within, the narratives of the past. (1990: 223)

The role of the media becomes increasingly important when nationalism goes through a period of transformation, as happens for example when the physical boundaries of the nation-state change or there is a need to include or exclude new people. However, globalization poses a new challenge to national identity. As Appadurai (1998: 8) observes, electronic media are able to promote not only national but transnational communities in their ability to cross borders. Tradionally the media served a national function that increasingly is no longer necessarily the case. This again underlines the importance of media and communications, and their contribution to the consequences of globalization.

In the case of all these families the question of identity is far from straightforward. The Finnish family experienced the awakening of national identity in the early twentieth century when Finland was still a part of Russia (Table 4.2). There was a mass movement against the 'Russification' of Finland, which resulted in resistance to everything that was considered Russian, especially everything with a symbolic meaning – such as language, media, money, stamps, flags. The independence movement underlined the differences between Russian and Finnish cultures and the homogeneity of Finnish culture. Finnish national identity was constructed, as often happens, in opposition to two neighbouring countries, Russia and Sweden ('We are not Swedish, we don't want to become Russians, let's be Finnish'). It was constructed on the relationship between geographical territory, language and culture, although with some difficulties because of the number of Swedish speakers in the country. As a result, when Finland gained its independence it became even more inward looking than before. Beyond the local identity, which the Finnish great-grandparents already had, the other identity that became available for them was a national one.

TABLE 4.2 Family 1: identity

	Great-grandmother Tyyne, 1905–87	Grandmother Eila, 1927–	Mother Terhi, 1953–	Son Nyrki, 1976–
Home country	Imperial Russia, Finland	Finland, EU citizenship from 1995	Finland, UK, EU citizenship from 1995	Finland, EU citizenship from 1995
Language spoken	Finnish	Finnish	Finnish	Finnish
Identity	Local, national	Local, national and cosmopolitan	Local and cosmopolitan	Local, national, cosmopolitan

As even the first generation of international communication theorists observed, media and communications mean more access. It is ironic in a way that when there is little or no access, there is less mediated connectivity, and the concerns of homogenization theorists are less valid. The Chinese great-grandfather Baosheng lived the most isolated life because he was poor and had no access to any media in the first half of his life. His culture was more homogeneous than that of the other two families and his access to other cultures came through the most violent kind of encounter, war. The foreign occupation made him aware, maybe for the first time in his life, of the difference between himself and the other, in this case the Japanese. At the same time it connected him more closely than ever before, beyond the local, with other Chinese people. If his identity was previously primarily local, it now became more national (Table 4.3).

TABLE 4.3 Family 2: identity

	Great-grandfather Baosheng, 1888–1971	Grandfather Zhansheng, 1923–2000	Father Qinghe 1944–	Son Junjie 1974–
Home country	China under Qing Dynasty until 1912, Republic of China 1912–49, Japanese occupation 1937–45, People's Republic of China 1949–	Republic of China 1912–49, Japanese occupation 1937–45, People's Republic of China 1949–	Republic of China 1912–49, Japanese occupation 1937–45, People's Republic of China 1949–	People's Republic of China 1949–
Language spoken	Chinese dialect	Chinese dialect	Chinese dialect	Chinese dialect
Identity	Chinese, peasant, local	Chinese, peasant, local	Chinese, local to national	Chinese, local to national to cosmopolitan

The only family which had formed another identity beyond the local and the national was the family in Zilupe (Table 4.4). Being at the same time Latvian and Jewish made them fully aware of the differences that were constructed in their national identity. Unlike the Finnish-speaking Lutheran Finns in their relationship to one Finnish identity, the Jewish family could never (even if they wished to) fully share in a single Latvian national identity. There was always another strong identity available to them which was not territory bound in the same way as the Chinese or the Finnish identities were constructed. However, it was longing to belong to a place, and resistance to oppressive national identity, that made grandfather Lasik leave for Palestine in search of a national space for Jewish people. Only

FIG 4.4 Nechemya as a soldier (second from right) in Bet Lid

TABLE 4.4 Family 3: identity

	Great-grandfather Moshe, 1881–1941	Grandfather Lasik, 1912–97	Father Nechemya, 1941–	Daughter Shani, 1972–
Home country	Latvia	Latvia, Palestine, Israel	Palestine, Israel	Israel
Languages spoken	Russian, Latvian, basic Hebrew (only for prayer purposes), Yiddish	Latvian, Russian, Hebrew, Yiddish	Hebrew	Hebrew, English
Identity	Jewish, Latvian	Jewish, Israeli, secular	Israeli, secular	Cosmopolitan and Israeli, secular

after he had moved to Palestine did he participate in the building of a unified national identity. Again, this process resulted in a turning inward, as exemplified by the grandfather's refusal to watch foreign films.

After the Communist Party took power in China in 1949 the country was closed down and disconnected from Taiwan, in the same way as there was a disconnection between Finland and Russia. In both cases, many people had to leave their country. While Antti's cousin fled to Soviet Russia, Junjie's uncle fled to Taiwan. There was no official communication

FIG 4.3 Shani as a soldier in Mitzpe Ramon

between Taiwan and China for 30 years. The uncle had no communication with his sister's family until the 1980s. As in many other communist countries, the national media and communications system was relatively easy to control. The less communication there is, the easier it is to control any national media and communications system, especially in the pre-electronic and digital era. Junjie's uncle could not visit, call or write letters to his sister's family for three decades.

When China started opening up in the 1980s, Western mass media products started flowing in. As in other post-communist countries (see, for example, Rantanen, 2002), these products have also been heavily criticized. The main theme of a Chinese bestseller, *China Can Say No* (1996) (and its sequels *China Still Says No* and *China Will Always Say No*), is 'just say no to American culture, ideology and value systems' (Burstein and de Keijzer, 1999: 181). In the 1990s the Chinese Communist Party sought to fuse traditional Marxism with nationalism. A sign of growing Chinese nationalism has been the revival of pride in Chinese culture. This has been seen in many areas, such as the attempt to give new life to traditional Chinese opera and other theatrical forms. It has also been expressed in renewed attention to morality and ethics derived from Confucianism, and in an emphasis on family values (Mackerras et al., 1998: 54–5). This influence can also be seen in our Chinese family, where the youngest family member listens both to Western pop music and to Chinese opera.

In this way, the earlier generations of these three families did not experience the direct influence of the media of another country. On the contrary, the media to which they had access primarily promoted nationalism. It was the national that became the most homogeneous, no matter what ideoscape (communism, nationalism, Zionism or a combination of them) it was based on. There is something in nationalism, especially at its highest stage, that makes it homogeneous, inward looking and closed. To be able to stay that way, it has to 'protect' itself from other cultures and reject cultural influences from outside. This 'protection' can only fully happen when media and communications are scarce and controlled by national authorities.

GLOBAL POPULAR CULTURE

According to Kivikuru (1988: 17), during the early decades of the twentieth century the Finnish media were, for the first time, heavily influenced by entertainment originating from the USA, including records, films and light entertainment. Even in the German-minded 1930s, American films became more popular in Finland. Quite frequently Sweden and Germany played the role of middlemen for the US cultural industry. Kivikuru writes that American jazz came to Finland through Germany, first as a word meaning 'everything new', and later in the form of music. However, during the war it was forbidden to listen to Allied 'enemy' stations (Finland was in the Axis coalition with Germany), and the Finnish grandmother Eila remembers her Swedish-speaking fellow students telling her after the war how they had secretly been listening to jazz on the BBC during the war. At the same time Eila and her sister Sisko were copying the lyrics of *Schlagers* (a German word for popular music), translated from German into Finnish, into their notebooks.

It was only in the 1960s that the big Anglo-American wave hit Finland, but it had already arrived in the 1950s in the form of books. As a child, Terhi read a lot of books, mainly translated from English, such as *Winnie the Pooh*, *The Little Princess*, *Little Lord Fauntleroy*, countless *Famous Five*, *Anne of Green Gables*, to mention just a few. She played with Audrey Hepburn and Elizabeth Taylor lookalike paper dolls, and cut out of newspapers and magazines pictures of members of the British Royal Family whose names she gave to the miniature people in her doll's house. She played with her best friend Ulla, whose dolls were named after the Iranian Royal Family of the time, the Pahlavis. She also spent endless hours in her grandparents' kiosk where they sold sweets, soft drinks, magazines – sitting on the floor and reading *Jerry Cotton*, *Tex Willer*, *Illustrated Classics* and other comic books. Later she became a subscriber to *Donald Duck* comic, which she received every week. Terhi remembers vividly the first television programmes 'Rin-Tin-Tin' and 'Lassie' shown on Finnish television in the 1960s. Her first television soap opera in the 1960s was also of US origin, 'Peyton Place', and she can still recall the names of its leading actors Mia Farrow and Ryan O'Neal. She also went regularly to the cinema, seeing films such as *Tarzan*, *Hatari* and numerous Elvis Presley movies in local cinemas that have now been closed. An Italian pop singer Robertino Lorentino was her first favourite, but then it was The Beatles for most of her teenage years. Terhi subscribed to a youth magazine called *Suosikki* and again cut out pictures of her favourite band. She only got her first, battery-operated, record player (after collecting tokens from Coca-Cola bottles) at the age of 14.

Shani, who spent 2 years in Turkey, returned to Israel having had early access to Western culture in the form of Barbie dolls and Smurfs, music and fashion long before her classmates in Israel. US mass culture arrived in Israel later, in the mid 1980s. This happened a generation later than in Finland, mainly because there was strong religious resistance to Western influence. Television was introduced to Israel only in 1968. As Katz writes establishment opposition to television after Israel was founded was manifold. There was the fear that book reading would decline; that newly developed Israeli culture and language, still in need of nurturing, would be swamped by imported, mostly US programmes; that national integration would be weakened by entertainment; and that politics would become less ideological, that is, less oriented to issues and more to charismatic personalities. The positive arguments for the introduction of television rested on nation-building and integration: absorption of immigrants, maintaining better contact with distant settlements and teaching the language (Katz, 1971: 253).[1]

However, after television was introduced, drama series consisted mainly of US and British imports. Usually, only one such series was aired at prime time. 'Kojak', 'Starsky and Hutch', 'Dallas', 'Dynasty' and the British dramatic serial 'Upstairs, Downstairs' may be listed among the most popular. 'Dallas' and 'Dynasty' were first aired on Channel 1. Five seasons of 'Dallas' were first shown in the early 1980s. After that came 'Dynasty'. At that time there was only Channel 1 in Israel, and naturally both shows became very popular. 'Dynasty' was rerun in early 1998.[2] The very same programmes were also shown on Finnish television and achieved high ratings among Finnish audiences.

For different reasons but with the same results, in this case because of strong Communist resistance, Junjie was the first in his family to have large-scale access to Western culture in the mid-1980s. This was the period when Western programmes started their major flow to Chinese television, including cartoons such as 'Mickey Mouse' and 'Donald Duck' and television drama series such as 'Dallas' and 'Falcon Crest' (Huang, 1994: 230) both shown in Finland and Israel. Junjie's first childhood memory, though, is of the time when he was 4 years old and saw a 'Donald Duck' cartoon on television in his home village. For him it was a collective experience, because his father worked in a factory which owned one black and white television set which was used to organize weekly outdoor TV viewings for villagers. Donald Duck spoke Chinese, since television programmes were dubbed, and a famous Chinese actor was the voice of Donald Duck. The four generations of the Chinese family first watched foreign films from other communist countries and Japan, which were favoured over Western films until the 1980s.

Junjie's next experience of Western culture was indeed in the 1980s, when as a high school student he started to read about it. The first music cassette he bought as a college student was 'Yesterday, Once More' by The Carpenters ('When I was young I'd listen to the radio, waitin' for my fav'rite songs') from 1973. He started to listen to Western music regularly, and The Beatles, Bob Dylan and John Denver became his favourites. China Radio International had at the time a very popular Western music programme Joy-FM, which Junjie also listened to. His favourite movie in the 1980s was Zorro, which he saw in his village. Chinese students considered Zorro a political hero because he fought for poor people in the countryside. Junjie had his first meal from McDonald's in 1997 when he was working as an intern at a television station.

Nyrki, from the youngest generation of the Finnish family, first became interested in music through his father's records, which included Bob Dylan and Finnish rock music. His first independent interest, very different from his father's musical taste, was US heavy metal music and bands such as Kiss, Twisted Sister, Wasp and Motley Crew. His 6 month stay in the USA in 1991 was to have a long-lasting impact on his musical taste, as he and his brother started listening to rap artists such as NWA, Public Enemy, and Ice-T. When they came back, they, like Shani with her Barbie dolls and Smurfs, had gained access to something that had not yet arrived in Finland in a big way. It is typical of all the family members who gained access to parts of US culture not yet accessible in their home country that they felt privileged compared with their friends. They did not feel that they had been influenced, and they even used that access to oppose the mainstream culture in their home country.

It is undeniable that some members of the second and third and all members of the fourth generation have been exposed to Western electronic media in a way that had never happened before. These Western media have mainly been of US and UK origin. This has happened at the same time as the spread of the English language. For the fourth generation of all three families, the only language besides their mother tongue is English. We see a considerable decline in knowledge of different languages if we compare the youngest generation of the Israeli and Finnish families with the previous generations of their families. The previous generations spoke more languages and they spoke different ones. These languages – even Swedish, the second official language of Finland – have now been replaced by English. English has also replaced German as the first foreign language at school. The Latvian great-grandfather Moshe spoke four languages in Zilupe, although, in contrast to his great-granddaughter with her formal higher education, he had little formal education. On the other hand, for the fourth generation of the Chinese family, English is the first and only foreign language ever spoken. For the Chinese family, it thus represents an increase in the number of languages known, while for the others it represents a decrease.

CONCLUSION

According to Tomlinson (1997: 175), one of the most ardent critics of cultural imperialism theory, there are still three reasons for assimilating cultural globalization to cultural imperialism: (1) the ubiquity of Western cultural goods; (2) the long history of Western imperialism; (3) the centrality of capitalism as a cultural influence. When we look at his first point, the ubiquity of Western cultural goods, we can see how rapidly these have spread in the last 30 years. Although Western imperialism has existed for a long time, its immediate influence in the cultural sphere has been relatively short. However, during that short period it has spread hand in hand with capitalism. We can look at any of our families and the lives of their members in different locations and see how Western cultural goods are now present in those locations, even if only in a mediated form.

One of the most important conclusions from this, then, is that the influence of American mass culture is relatively young, having only been felt during the last 50 years. Only the two youngest generations of the Finnish family have been surrounded by American mass culture from their earliest childhood. In the two other families, it started even later. Shani was influenced by it only because she lived abroad. Junjie was already a student when the big wave hit him. For the older generations, the influence has been much shorter and much more strongly counteracted by homogeneous nationalism.

In a way, access to Western culture through media and communications has opened up a new space to those who either can afford it or have sufficient knowledge to use it. Many members of our families gained this access through their education or through emigration (even if temporary) earlier than most people in their countries. However, the youngest generation in Finland has now gained this access without higher education. Since English is now taught in Finland from the second grade, and because of the availability and affordability of media and communication in Finland, the majority of Finns have access, if they wish, to Anglo-American cultural products. The same products are available in Helsinki, London, Tel Aviv and Beijing almost simultaneously. One does not have to travel to gain access to them, because this access comes through connectivity. The door has been opened to Western products in a way that has never happened before.

Despite availability and affordability, the consequence has not yet been global homogenization. The strongest homogenizing factor so far has been nationalism. Each of our families and each of their members have been influenced by nationalism. In some cases this has worked against them, as it did against the Latvian great-grandfather Moshe when he was denied citizenship rights because of his religion. In other cases, the members of these families have actively and voluntarily contributed to this access, as did the Israeli grandfather Lasik and the Finnish great-grandfather Antti. Even now, each member of our families would define him/herself primarily in terms of his/her nationality. After 6 years in the UK, Terhi would define herself as a Finn living in London, not as Finnish-British or as an EU citizen.

It is impossible to discuss homogenization without discussing heterogenization. Whenever I have referred in this chapter to homogenization it has been impossible not to refer also to heterogenization. Sometimes what is homogenization for one person is heterogenization for another. It is possible to understand the complicated nature of the relationship between the two only by looking at both of them and seeing how they are connected.

NOTES

1 www.museum.tv/archives/etv/Ihtm1l/israel/israel.htm, 8 August 2003.
2 http://www.angelfire.com/il/ILTV/Oldies.html#DaDy, 8 July 2003.

5 HETEROGENIZATION

Whilst Sreberny's (1996) second-generation media and communication theorists talked about homogenization as globalization's main (if not only) consequence, the next generation of culture, media and globalization theorists argue for different outcomes, using such concepts as heterogenization, hybridization, fuzziness, *mélange*, cut-and-mix, criss-cross and crossover. For example, for Pieterse (1995: 49) and Rowe and Schelling (1991: 231), globalization is hybridization, 'the way in which forms become separated from existing practices and recombine with new forms in new practice'. (Rowe and Schelling, 1991:231). The third-generation globalization theorists were not economists or political scientists, but anthropologists or scholars in the newly emerging field of cultural studies who had done their fieldwork and interviews. They were not interested in the politics or economics of media, but in how people used the media. They saw their audiences as active and able to resist the power of the global media. Audiences tend to 'naturally gravitate towards programming choices that appear most relevant or "proximate" to their own context and thus allow them to seek the pleasure of recognition of their own culture' (Straubhaar, 1991, cited in Chadha and Kavoori, 2000: 425), or 'ultimately people like to see something close to their lives' (Hong, 1998, cited in Chadha and Kavoori, 2000: 425) instead of surrounding themselves with Western media.

The contrast between the two approaches, homogenization and heterogenization, is clearly exemplified by the way in which two scholars, Hamelink and Lull, present their identical observations, only to reach exactly opposite conclusions. Hamelink (1983) uses the concept of cultural synchronization. He writes:

> In a Mexican village the traditional ritual dance precedes a soccer match, but the performance features a gigantic Coca-Cola bottle.
> In Singapore, a band dressed in traditional Malay costume offer a heart-breaking imitation of Fats Domino.
> In Saudi Arabia, the television station performs only one local cultural function – the call for the Moslem prayer. Five times a day, North American cops and robbers yield to the traditional muezzin.
> In its gigantic advertising campaign, IBM assures Navajo Indians that their cultural identity can be effectively protected if they use IBM typewriters equipped with the Navajo alphabet. (1983: 56)

Hamelink writes that 'one conclusion still seems unanimously shared: the impressive variety of the world's cultural systems is waning due to a process of cultural synchronization that is without any historic precedent. Never before has the process of cultural influence proceeded so subtly, without any blood being shed and with the receiving culture thinking it had sought such cultural influence.' The difference between this and Lull's (2000) conclusion with regard to global cultural mix is remarkable. Lull writes:

> A Peruvian band playing traditional Andes folk music at a tourist restaurant in Playa del Carmen, Mexico, suddenly breaks into the English band Queen's 'We will rock you' to the delight of German and Canadian girls in the audience.
> The Milan collection of lamps sold in the United States are made in Taiwan and distributed by a French wholesaler.
> More than 400 million people worldwide, in countries including Russia, Tunisia, Zimbabwe, and Switzerland, regularly watch TV soap operas that originate in Spanish-language nations.
> A German pop music band travels to the United States where they perform solely for Vietnamese-American immigrants who use the music to unite their community. (2000: 232–3)

For Lull, globalization does not mean some universal, technology-based super-society that covers the globe and destroys local social systems and cultures. 'Despite technology's awesome reach,' he writes, 'we have not, and will not, become one people' (2000: 233). As a result, we have two conflicting conclusions. This is very much the situation we are in now and have been in for 10 years or so. There seems to be no way out: you are either for or against globalization, depending on what you think about its consequences. This simply closes the discussion and prevents us from seeing further.

NEW WAYS OF THINKING ABOUT HOMOGENIZATION AND HETEROGENIZATION

But what if there are flaws in the thinking of both homogenization and heterogenization schools with regard to the consequences of globalization? The faults of the homogenization theorists have already been introduced in the previous chapter: they have primarily to do with the unit of analysis, that is society or nation-state. Criticism of the heterogenization school has mainly been directed at: (1) the power it gives to the audience; (2) its neglect of the economic power held by global media firms; (3) its neglect of the fact that the biggest media companies are located mainly in the USA; and (4) its neglect of inequality of access of members of the audience to media and communications.

Thinking about the communication process has very much relied on a one-way model, where information goes through one channel, from sender to receiver, with some possible feedback. This model, with its different variations (McQuail and Windahl, 1993), has dominated the field in media and communications studies in both the UK and the USA. What has happened with the emergence of media and cultural studies has been the 'unpacking' of the audience, which has shown a variety of ways in which people receive and interpret messages. This has happened in communication, media and cultural studies. There is a widely held view that no homogeneous audience exists any longer, only a fragmented audience with distinctive tastes. This has been a great achievement of works of scholarship since World War II, when the dominant theory was one of powerful media that could change audience behaviour.

However, the starting point for these studies has been national audiences with distinctive, homogeneous tastes. Even in studies such as that of Liebes and Katz (1990) on the reception of 'Dallas', different national groups were compared with one another. These cross-national studies were the legacy of international communication studies. As a result, what we see are differences between national audiences, not within national audiences. The next step could be to compare different groups within national audiences with other equivalent groups within other national audiences. Studies on diasporic groups have already indicated that huge differences exist within national audiences (Gillespie, 1995; Georgiou, 2001). As Gillespie (1995: 6) points out, the term 'diaspora' is useful as an intermediate concept between the local and the global. But it goes even further: diasporas challenge the way we think about nation-states and their homogeneity.

We may find that similarities also exist across borders within non-diasporic groups. For example, young urban professionals all over the world watch similar TV programmes (such as 'Friends') irrespective of their nationality and location, whereas their parents watch entirely different programmes, very often of an exclusively national nature. In my previous work on the media in post-communist Russia (Rantanen, 2002) I concluded that different media are open to globalization in different ways. While old media (such as newspapers or radio) are often more national in their orientation, new media such as video or the Internet are much more global. Homogenization theorists still claim that global media companies, which are located mainly in the United States, transmit homogeneous messages that are delivered throughout the world with similar effects. However, these effects do not necessarily have to do with the content of these messages; they may promote adaptation of the general framework for production. Herman and McChesney (1997: 8–9) list as the consequences of globalization: (1) larger cross-border flows of media output; (2) the growth of media TNCs; (3) the tendency toward centralization of media control; and (4) the spread and intensification of commercialization. They see the primary effect of the globalization process – the manifestation of the strength of the great powers and the TNCs whose interests they serve – to be the implantation of the commercial model of communication. The commercial model then creates a 'culture of entertainment' that is, according to Herman and McChesney, incompatible with a democratic order.

The heterogenization school, on the other hand, claims that the messages may be homogeneous and originate from the West, but they do not have similar effects. To support their argument they have developed concepts such as de-territorialization and indigenization.

POSSIBLE CONSEQUENCES I: DE-TERRITORIALIZATION

Several researchers have talked about 'de-territorialization', the loss of the 'natural' relation of culture to geographical and social territories, where there is no longer necessarily any connection between identity and locality (see, for example, Morley and Robins, 1995: 87). Researchers have also used the term 're-territorialization' to designate a situation in which people attempt to re-establish a new cultural 'home' wherever they go (Tomlinson, 1999: 148) or to fuse imported traditions with resources in the new territory to create local versions of distant cultures (Lull, 2000: 253). Both are useful terms when we are trying to analyse what happens to identity in the era of globalization, especially as a result of the effect of media and communications.

If de-territorialization takes place, what then are the consequences? In the previous chapter, I raised the question of which is more homogeneous, globalization or nationalism. During the last 100 years, nationalism has been one of the most powerful ideoscapes. It has, of course, been in competition with religions and with different political ideologies, especially socialism. Emerging globalization, like any other movement or ideology in history, has not been a coherent and homogeneous phenomenon. However, unlike previous movements or ideologies, its speed and spread have been faster than we have seen before. The most important challenge for research is to try to identify factors and circumstances where globalization changes existing practices. As Barker (1997: 191–2) has observed, globalization has increased the range of sources and resources available for the construction of identity, allowing the production of hybrid identities in the context of a post-traditional global society where, although bounded societies and states are very much still with us, the circulation of other global cultural discourses cuts across them.

If globalization is understood as increasing the symbolic sources or resources available to people, it can also been seen as an escape from the prison of nationalism. As Appadurai has noted, 'one man's imagined community is another man's political prison' (1990: 295). This conclusion is very different from that of homogenization theorists, who see globalization as a threat to national identities. However, the situation is not this simple. It would be too easy to see globalization only as a force for liberation from a national prison. Globalization also invites resistance, and this resistance often appears in the form of nationalism. Resistance is often seen purely in terms of progress, as in anti-globalization movements, but sometimes this resistance is extremely reactionary and even dangerous. When cultural identities associated with nation-states start to decline, it is almost impossible to predict the outcome. Hall (1991) was one of the first academics to acknowledge the role of media and communications in this process. He writes:

> In cultural terms, the new kind of globalization has to do with a new form of global mass culture, very different from that associated with [English] identity, and the cultural identities associated with the nation-state in an earlier phase. Global mass culture is dominated by the modern means of cultural production, dominated by the image which crosses and re-crosses linguistic frontiers much more rapidly and more easily, and which speaks languages in a much more immediate way. It is dominated by all the ways in which the visual and graphic arts have entered directly into the reconstitution of popular life, of entertainment and of leisure. It is dominated by television and by film, and by the image, imagery, and styles of mass advertising. (1991; 27)

Hall (1996: 619) writes that three things can happen as a consequence of globalization: (1) as a result of cultural homogenization, national identities are eroded; (2) national or 'local' identities are strengthened by resistance to globalization; (3) although national identities may be declining, new identities are formed.

Contrary to many expectations, national identities have not been eroded. Rather, we have actually witnessed the creation of 'new' national identities in many parts of the world, especially in Central and Eastern Europe after the collapse of communism. What we have witnessed recently is resistance to globalization, in the form either of religion (such as Islamic fundamentalism) or of nationalism. Globalization can actually contribute to increasing nationalism, as has happened in post-communist Russia (Rantanen, 2002). National and local identities are not only being strengthened, but also being created. What we have also seen are new, very aggressive forms of 'national' identity based on language, ethnicity or religion and very intolerant of people who do not fit in. Hall saw this as early as 1991, when he wrote:

> All I want to say about that is, that when the era of nation-states in globalization begins to decline, one can see a regression to a very defensive and highly dangerous form of national identity which is driven by a very aggressive form of racism. (1991: 26)

This view is very different from that of the media imperialism school, which viewed national identities as threatened by cultural imperialism.

This school of thought often took a romantic view of nationalism as something appreciated and shared by everybody, ignoring such features as language, ethnicity and religion, which separate people within every nation-state (Chadha and Kavoori, 2000: 417). In fact, these elements imprison people who are excluded from a nation-state because they do not share the features characteristic of the majority. For these people, globalization is more of a salvation than a threat; they may welcome a new nation-state if it removes their second-class citizen status. Others, often the majority within a particular nation-state, do see globalization as a threat, especially if it seems to attack traditional values.

New identities, which are not based on nationalism, are also emerging. These are facilitated by messages and images that cross frontiers, often supporting some characteristic which is suppressed by a particular nation-state (such as sexual orientation or religion) or that is new (any new ideology, image or invention). Many of these new identities are supported by media and communications which connect people, wherever their location. The rest – whether connection becomes a shared experience – is up to them. New identities have emerged everywhere, not only in the West. However, one of the most widespread identities is that of the consumer (Sklair, 2002). This identity, like many others, can serve different purposes. In some historical instances, such as before the collapse of communism, it functioned as an oppositional identity when people wanted access to goods which their government was not willing to give them. In other historical instances, globalization only imposes consumerism when people in different non-places around the world buy the same things. It becomes a mass movement without cause, as after Christmas in Western countries when mobs of people flock to buy things at a discounted price in the annual 'sales'.

POSSIBLE CONSEQUENCES II: INDIGENIZATION

Tomlinson (1999: 128–30) has criticized the use of the term 'de-territorialization' for two reasons. One is that it is based on the myth of the pre-modern localism of closed and isolated cultures that never existed, even before electronic globalization. Tomlinson (1991: 130–1) also points out the uneven character of de-territorialization, and here he refers to the power of US and UK media companies compared with others. De-territorialization, according to Tomlinson, is not a two-way street but has elements of cultural subordination.

De-territorialization does not help us understand how it takes place, but rather confirms the state of affairs. Appadurai (1998) further clarifies the difference between the two approaches, homogenization and heterogenization, by using the term *indigenization*. He writes:

Claims of creeping global homogenization invariably subspeciate into either an argument about Americanization, or an argument about commoditization, and very often these two arguments are very closely linked. What these arguments fail to consider is that at least as rapidly as forces from the various metropolises are brought into new societies, they tend to become indigenized in one way or another: this is true of music and housing styles as much as it is true of science and terrorism, spectacles and constitutions. (1998: 32)

The idea of indigenization helps to explain *how* heterogenization occurs. Lull uses the concept of transculturation, which he defines as 'a process whereby cultural forms literally move through time and space where they interact with other cultural forms and settings, influence each other, produce new forms, change cultural settings and produce cultural hybrids – the fusing of cultural forms' (2000: 242–3). Transculturation is very close to de-territorialization, the loss of the 'natural' relation between culture and geographic and social territory, the release of cultural signs from fixed locations in space and time, and the disembedding (lifting out) of people and symbolic forms from the places where we expect them to be (Giddens, 1990: 21).

The problem with these definitions is that they use passive forms and it is not entirely clear who is the agent of indigenization or transculturation. If we look at media and communications and their role in this process, at least three alternatives are possible. First, global media companies may indigenize their own products. This may be either by producing products that have a global appeal as such, or by hiring people with multicultural backgrounds and/or knowledge of the markets at which the products are targeted. These products are thus already indigenized when they enter the market. For example, one could argue that media companies in the USA and the UK have been able to create cultural products designed for global markets. The second option is that national media companies indigenize global products. They buy, for example, TV programme formats which they then indigenize by using domestic actors, as has happened with programmes such as 'Big Brother' or 'Who Wants To Be a Millionaire?'. National media companies also indigenize programmes just by translating them into national languages, using voiceover or subtitles, or by finding a domestic singer to perform a piece of music that has been produced and performed somewhere else. The third option is that the audience itself indigenizes cultural products.

In the past, national, often public, broadcasting companies acted as filters between global media products and local audiences. This was possible because in many countries the state was able to control access to technology by regulating the domestic market. It did this not only for altruistic reasons to protect its home market, but also because it had its own interests in constructing and promoting the national. Increasingly, the role of national broadcasting companies has diminished because of the transformation in the audiovisual landscape. Sinclair et al. (1996) list four reasons for this change: (1) technology's capacity to deliver across frontiers; (2) increasing commercialization; (3) the demand for programmes from new sources; and (4) increasing dependence on the USA.

What we see here is a complex combination of the global and the national. As Robertson (1995: 29–31) wrote in a famous article, the consequence of globalization is neither homogenization nor heterogenization, neither global nor local, but rather simultaneous, mutually implicative, complementary and interpenetrative glocalization. I have argued elsewhere (Rantanen, 2002) that the process does not happen between the global and the local, but between the global and the national. While global companies have started to 'nationalize' their products, national companies have started to globalize their products, that is, to make their domestic products more global in order to attract both domestic and global markets. Even audiences, or rather individuals in audiences, no longer accept the role of national filters, but use their technological and cultural knowledge to gain direct access to cultural products wherever they are produced.

The concept of indigenization can be used at various stages of the process: (1) to analyse how global media companies indigenize their products for national and local markets; (2) to analyse how national media companies indigenize their products for national audiences; and (3) to analyse how audiences indigenize these products. Seen in this way, the process of indigenization is already present in the production and distribution process. There is some similarity between the homogenization and heterogenization schools in their analysis of indigenization. Kivikuru described modelling the process whereby 'foreign influences are often gradually partly "domesticated" or transformed in order to fit better to the cultural climate' (1988: 13). Kivikuru, as a homogenization theorist, uses this concept to analyse dependency as 'a direct or indirect external, non-reciprocal influence on the mass communication system, production and distribution arrangements, ownership, media content and culture, singly or together' (1988: 13). The strength of her argument is that she pays attention to the process of domestication. The weakness of her argument is that domestication is only seen as a form of adoption or absorption. For homogenization theorists there is no resistance and audiences play no role in their analysis.

This intensification of complex connectivity, as Tomlinson (1999: 1) calls it, becomes clearer when we look at the four generations of our three families. We can see similarities and dissimilarities between them in relation to the effects of globalization, depending on their access to media and communications which gradually becomes a decisive factor.

THE FIRST GENERATIONS

TABLE 5.1 Family 1: ideology and resistance

	Great-grandmother Tyyne, 1905–87	Grandmother Eila, 1927–	Mother Terhi, 1953–	Son Nyrki, 1976–
Ideology	Lutheran, agrarian, voted regularly	Social democrat, secular non-partisan, votes regularly	Disillusioned leftist, no longer interested in party politics, does not vote, secular but member of the Finnish Lutheran Church	Green, not interested in party politics but votes occasionally, secular
Resistance to	Communism, Soviet Union, idleness and drunkenness	Communism, Soviet Union, women's unequal pay, idleness and drunkenness	War in Vietnam 1961–75, Chilean coup 1973, Cold War, patriarchy, drunkenness, idleness	Compulsory national military service Protestant work ethic

If we consider the members of our three families in the late nineteenth and early twentieth centuries, their access to media and communication was very different. The Finnish great-grandmother Tyyne, and the Chinese great-grandfather Baosheng primarily lived their lives locally without changing place. The Chinese family had no access to any media, and the Finnish family had access only to newspapers, which came out three times a week. It was only when Tyyne and her husband Antti lost their farm and had to move to Kotka that they gained access to electronic media.

This was also the time of the first de- and re-territorialization for the Finnish family (Table 5.1). Their culture was no longer connected to one place, as it had been in Juva; they had to adjust to and absorb a new urban culture, which replaced their agrarian way of life. However, they maintained their connection to their old way of life by visiting their relatives and by writing to them and later phoning them. They also reacted to the new way of life, accepting only some of its elements. They rejected the communality of the working-class culture and ideology and maintained their former individual and political identity. They were not workers, but small entrepreneurs. The processes of re- and de-territorialization took place at the same time, and they 'solved' the contradiction between the two ways of life by combining them.

Their identity, which had earlier been primarily local, now became more national. It is often said in Finland that the Winter War of 1939–40 united Finnish people across class and cultural differences. It also contributed to the construction of a national identity, which included a myth about Finns forming the last frontier between the mythical 'West' and 'East', and Finns' solitary duty to protect the 'West'. For the Finnish family, as for many other families of the world, the first major encounter with globalization was a violent one: a physical threat of invasion. The Finnish grandfather's second 'journey' abroad was when he went as a member of the Finnish army to invade parts of the Soviet Union. Finland also became an ally of Germany, and German troops arrived in Finland in 1941.

Globalization at this time was thus almost entirely related to military intrusions and exclusions. This experience remained with the oldest generation of the Finnish family for the rest of their lives as their primary encounter with globalization. It also affected their daughters who, for 4 years of their childhood, were separated from their father and lived in fear of his death, as well as of their own, as they sought refuge in bomb shelters.

TABLE 5.2 Family 2: ideology and resistance

	Great-grandfather Baosheng, 1888–1971	Grandfather Zhansheng, 1923–2000	Father Qinghe, 1944–	Son Junjie, 1974–
Ideology	Traditional Confucianism	Taoism and Confucianism	Socialism and a fan of Chairman Mao, atheist	Liberal cosmopolitan with a strong Chinese national identity, disappointed with any ideology Previously an atheist like his father but now his attitude to religion has been gradually changed to be more tolerant to different religions His mother also believes in Taoism
Resistance to		Foreign television programmes, any advertisement on the television	Capitalism	Inequality, cynical about all current social systems

The Chinese great-grandfather Baosheng first gained access to the media only through the loudspeakers installed by the government in his village towards the end of his life. It is fair to say that the members of his generation primarily lived their lives locally and their access to global media was limited (Table 5.2). Their main encounter with the other was again a violent one: a foreign army occupied their country and they had to go into hiding. This experience made the Chinese family, like their Finnish counterparts, lean more on their national identity.

TABLE 5.3 Family 3: ideology and resistance

	Great-grandfather Moshe, 1881–1941	Grandfather Lasik, 1912–97	Father Nechemya, 1941–	Daughter Shani, 1972–
Ideology	Jewish non-Zionist, strong identification with the local Jewish community in which he lived all his life	Local socialist, patriotic	Liberal	Cosmopolitan with a sense of Israeli national identity
Resistance to	Did not approve his son's decision to leave Latvia and join the 'Aliyah' in Israel (driven by Zionist ideology)	Capitalism/hedonism, opposed to fundamental orthodox religious Jewish	Anti-right-wing, anti militarism opposed to fundamental orthodox religious Jewish	Anti-right-wing, anti-colonialist (particularly in the Israeli context), opposed to fundamental orthodox religious Jewish

The Latvian great-grandfather Moshe was already urban and middle class and thus able to enjoy various media much earlier than his Chinese and Finnish counterparts. He also, unlike them, had a dual identity: Jewish and Latvian (Table 5.3). His Jewish identity was not place-bound in the same way as his Latvian identity. His family's identity had been de- and re-territorialized several times over the centuries. Living in the borderland between Latvia, Russia and Belarus, he was able to mix and match, and was capable of dealing with different identities. However, because of his dual identity, he was never fully accepted as an equal subject and suffered discrimination.

THE SECOND GENERATIONS

The Latvian grandfather Lasik in Zilupe wanted to recombine territory and culture and decided to emigrate. His father Moshe, disapproved of his son's decision to leave for Palestine and remained in his home town until he died there at the hands of German troops. Hence, like that of his Chinese counterpart, Moshe's life was lived very locally, although his was an urban life. His son Lasik was the first member of any of the three families to change his life fundamentally by changing places, when he left for Palestine, which he only knew from reading literature and newspapers and attending meetings. Here we see a first form of global de-territorialization with a dramatic outcome: a change of place not within one country, but from one country to another. He was willing to leave his comfortable, urban middle-class lifestyle and change it for a communitarian agricultural way of life. This emigration had nothing to do with economics, but was solely based on ideology and religion. He also moved despite his parents' disapproval.

His decision was also based on imagination, on a dream of something better than what was available in Latvia. His image of Israel was partly imaginary – a historical, even mythical, picture of a country once called Israel which had very little to do with the actual circumstances in Palestine. Of course, he must have known something of this from the letters of people who had already emigrated and from newspapers and literature available from Jewish immigration organizations. But the idea of an 'empty' land was false, just as it was for emigrants to North America and Australia. What he and his fellow emigrants encountered was resistance from Palestinian people who had no intention of de- or re-territorializing their culture and resisted the settlers' attempts to take over the land they considered theirs.

What we see here is not de- or re-territorialization, but emigration as an escape from circumstances which, for personal or political reasons, were unsatisfactory. The Jewish emigrants from Latvia did not try to re-territorialize their culture, since their culture was not territory-bound. Theirs was a conscious decision to leave behind their former home countries, the culture that they had found oppressive, and even their language, and instead to start speaking Hebrew. Although Hebrew is one of the oldest languages in the world, it was only adopted as a spoken language by Jewish immigrants in Palestine from the 1880s.[1] They even discarded their old names for new Israeli names. What Jewish emigrants took with them from their home countries was their religion and ideology, which they sought to re-territorialize. This was a much more dramatic change than that experienced by the members of the Finnish family who moved within their own country: it was a move in the opposite direction (from urban to agriculture), and the break was much more dramatic and complete. There was no opportunity to go back and visit, and even communication was limited to occasional letters, which took a long time to arrive. We see a process of heterogenization in the early days of kibbutzim, where people from different countries, often not even sharing the same language, started to live together. Different immigrant groups had their own newspapers, which reflected their political, religious and ethnic identities. This heterogenization then became a process of homogenization in the name of national ideology.

The heterogenization of the early days was soon to become homogenization, as the new language, religion and culture were introduced. The resistance to the new state of Israel, whether from Palestinians or from other countries involved, made the new communities even more inward looking. The creation of the new was a rejection, a closing of doors on the old. We can see the same phenomenon in Finland after the country gained its independence in 1917, and in China after 1949. Nationalism, in its early stages, breeds homogeneity and inwardness. It rejects all elements that do not fit in. The young Latvian man had now become an Israeli citizen who gradually became more and more suspicious of anything that was new and came from outside. He sought to maintain and project the values he believed in: communitarianism and equality within his own community. He refused to see foreign films shown in the kibbutz cinema and did not want access to modern media.

The Finnish family was exposed for the first time to electronic media when they moved to the town of Kotka. However, their access to the media was restricted. For example, their radio listening was family listening and happened only at certain times, usually in the evenings and on Sundays when at least one of the parents was at home. The programmes they listened to were domestically produced radio shows whose format was imported. Although their radio use was not communal in the same way as in the Chinese village after World War II or in the Israeli kibbutz, the paper mill used bulletin boards and oral communication to inform its members – and there was the paper mill whistle which told its workers when shifts began and ended.

In a way, although the Finnish family left their isolated agrarian lifestyle behind, they came to live in a community knit as closely (if not closer) than their agrarian community, and controlled by the strict working hours of the paper mill. Listening to one national broadcasting channel and reading a local newspaper did not open up their world beyond the national. This was a time when nationhood was still being built in a country which had achieved its independence only two decades earlier. Even in this very closed and homogeneous country, globalization could be experienced through ethnoscapes: Eila remembers seeing her first foreigners in Kotka where Swedish and Norwegian guest workers were employed to install the new machinery at the paper mill. Still, the Finnish family's transculturation was national, not global. It was only when they moved to Kotka, a small town, that they began to regularly see foreign films.

Eila who, unlike her parents, had gained a medium of communication beyond the national by studying foreign languages, yearned for escape from the small-town mentality and access to a wider world. She became a journalist and travelled widely, although she ultimately returned to her home town. She has many identities: agrarian, urban and – going one step further than her parents – capital city dweller. She remains very place-bound, but that does not prevent her from being a keen traveller. After retiring she seriously considered buying a house in Spain, as many Finns have done. Ultimately, she has a strong Finnish national identity that is very much based on those crucial years when her country was at war.

The Chinese family's second generation also encountered nationalism after the People's Republic was founded. In their case, it was also something that divided the family: the uncle who had fought on the 'wrong side' escaped to Taiwan. The political situation between the two countries meant that contacts between the family members in the two Chinas were cut for more than 40 years. They were all Chinese, but citizens of different countries. The isolation policy restricted not only travel and immigration, but also media and communications. The government policy of installing loudspeakers in villages, through which its messages were delivered, also meant that it could effectively control the content of the messages. As in the case of Israel, it was reaching inwards rather than outwards.

The process of de- and re-territorialization also touched the Chinese family, but again in a different form. Communism, as a global ideology, was first introduced to China from abroad, but then indigenized into a Chinese version. It added another element to people's identities: they were not only citizens of a country, but also members of the wider global community of communist countries and parties. This was a communist version of globalization which emphasized global solidarity with other like-minded people, but at the same time, although acknowledging that even in the West there were people who were sympathetic to their cause, closing its doors to Western countries. The communist international movement reached across frontiers, but was also divided into national movements, which were sometimes in serious conflict with each other.

THE THIRD GENERATIONS

Whilst the members of the first and second generations all encountered war, that was not necessarily the case with the third generations. The third generations of the Finnish and Chinese families have so far been able to live in a situation in which they have not experienced war personally. For them, war has become familiar through the mass media and especially television. This has not been the case for the Israeli family, whose members' experience of war is direct as well as mediated.

If the absence of war unites the Chinese and Finnish experiences, emigration and travel separates them. The Finnish grandmother Eila started to travel abroad soon after the 1939–45 war, and the next generation followed her example. Eila came home from her assignments abroad as a journalist full of stories to tell to her daughter Terhi. The mother's and the daughter's lives were very much tied to world news events: when something newsworthy happened, Eila had to go to work. Terhi still remembers vividly when the US President John F. Kennedy was shot in 1963 when she was 10 years old, because of her mother's urgent departure for work. Most of her global experience as a child was still mediated, mainly by the pulp fiction sold in her grandparents' kiosk, and by films, but increasingly by television. After she had passed her entrance exam to secondary school at the age of 10, her mother took her abroad for the first time, to Sweden, a neighbouring country. When she was 14 years old she and her mother went together for two weeks to Romania. At the age of 16 she travelled for the first time independently, but with a group, to Leningrad (St Petersburg) in the then Soviet Union. All these trips were quite typical at the time. Sweden has traditionally been a popular destination (Finland was once part of Sweden) and was culturally close (Finland is a bilingual country, with Swedish as its second official language). The Soviet Union was another neighbouring country, which Finns frequently visited, and Romania was an early mass tourism destination for Finns.

Despite her mother's stories and her visits abroad, which were more numerous and took place earlier than those of previous generations of her family, Terhi's outlook on life was very national. Her childhood was still full of stories about Finland's heroic fight against the Soviet Union, her grandfather and his friends getting drunk and talking about the war, her

FIG 5.1 Eila reading a Disney book to Terhi in Helsinki

teacher showing the places in her home town bombed by the Russians. Finns were supposed to feel superior to every other country, to their neighbouring countries and especially to the Soviet Union, the country to which Finland had lost the war. They were also supposed to have qualities nobody else had, such as the much celebrated and mythical Finnish *sisu* (guts). Terhi's outlook on life was about to change completely, with images and sounds brought by the mass media from countries whose existence she barely knew of.

This happened as she entered her teens when Finnish television, like television in many countries, began to transmit reports and images of the famine in Biafra, the invasion of Czechoslovakia, the war in Vietnam and the Chilean coup. These events, happening far away in countries she had never visited, took her onto the streets to demonstrate. She still remembers how a policeman hit her with his baton and how an elderly lady who supported the Shah of Iran hit her with her handbag when she took part in a demonstration against the Shah's visit to Helsinki. She remembers shouting slogans such as 'Ho, Ho, Ho Chi Minh' (the name of the Vietnamese political leader) and learning her first phrases of Spanish when she shouted 'El pueblo unido, jamás sera vencido' ('united people cannot be beaten') with her fellow demonstrators against the military junta which took power in Chile in 1973. She had no first-hand knowledge of these countries, but she was on the streets demonstrating against what she perceived as injustice. The first foreigners she established friendships with in Finland were Chilean refugees, with whom she started speaking English, the only language they could share.

Terhi's participation was based on information and images she received through the media. Her participation was in no way unique: she was influenced by the radical students and youth movement, which took young people onto the streets in many countries. It was simply one of the most dominant ideoscapes of that time, which was greatly accelerated by media and communications. Terhi had never seen a starving child or a human being shot before television brought these pictures into her home.

The radical movement in Finland took a national turn and was again indigenized in a similar way to communism in China. In Finland, unlike in many other Western countries, many members of the radical youth movement became orthodox communists, much inspired and influenced by the Soviet Union. This was a reaction against the previous generation's hostility to the Soviet Union, the glorification of the war and the acceptance of the military alliance with Nazi Germany. It temporarily brought many members of that generation into the process of communist globalization, which included only communist countries and 'progressive' forces in the West. This movement died even before the collapse of communism, but momentarily connected young people on both sides of the Iron Curtain.

In a less distinctive way, but again rejecting the choices of the previous generation, the Israeli father Nechemya left the kibbutz to which his father

Lasik had given all his efforts. He reached out not only to urban life in Israel, but to other countries as well. He left not because he had to, but because it offered him a chance to do new things. Terhi did the same in her career as an academic, a couple of years here and there abroad, but always returning to Finland. Unlike many migrant workers, they are educated middle-class people who know the language of the country they go to, or speak English as their working language, and are able to sell their intellectual capital across frontiers.

Nechemya returned to Israel where he now works, but Terhi is now living in the UK where she is married to a British academic and works in academia. She encounters almost daily the question of where she is from, since her accent reveals that she is not British. Terhi still has a Finnish passport, but has also started applying for British citizenship. Her plan is to have dual citizenship, since Finland has accepted this. In her case, this is not an issue of great importance, since she is an EU citizen, but she wants British citizenship as a way of expressing her dual identity.

How is Terhi's dual identity expressed in her everyday life? She tries to live her life in two countries, in the way Beck calls polygamy, with access to many worlds. Her daily life in London is very much that of a British academic working in a British higher education institution, where most of her colleagues are British, but most of the students are from overseas. She feels 'at home' at work with her students, because they are outsiders in British society in the same way as she feels she is. On the other hand, she does not feel an outsider in London, a global city where so many are in a similar situation to hers. She also uses media and communications daily to maintain contact with her culture, family and friends in Finland.

At best, Terhi thinks that she is extremely privileged to have access to several countries, cultures and languages. At worst, she feels she does not belong anywhere, but falls between countries. Most of her problems have to do with languages: she is afraid of losing her fluent command of Finnish, but she can never become a native speaker of English. In social situations she also struggles with her inclination not to speak and to withdraw rather than to perform. Her husband calls her a hermit, lacking the basic social skills that are such an essential feature of British middle-class culture. She consoles herself by remembering how a world-famous Finnish composer living in Los Angeles said in an interview that he found himself at parties mostly talking to a palm tree. Terhi wishes that there were more palm trees in London to talk to.

In Terhi's case she has not de- or re-territorialized her culture, but rather kept her two lives quite separate from each other. Owing to her regular visits to Finland and her access to media and communications, she has not had to abandon her culture completely like our Israeli grandfather. And she does not want to.

THE FOURTH GENERATION

In the Chinese family, it was Junjie who was the first to leave as a result of his access to education and to the English language, in the same way as earlier generations of the other families did. Junjie remembers that he saw his first foreigners at the age of 15 when his aunt took him to see a car race whose participants were foreigners. Junjie stood at the side of the highway, saw these foreign cars speeding by and caught glimpses of the drivers' faces. He says that the biggest change in his life happened when he moved from his home village to the capital. Compared with his home village, Beijing was a global city in which he had access to media and communications and to an urban lifestyle. Unlike the members of the Finnish family, where changes have taken place generation by generation, Junjie moved from a small village to a capital city and then to global cities. All this has happened within 10 years.

Junjie has crossed not only geographical but also mental frontiers. A village boy raised in a local school according to the doctrine of Chairman Mao, he followed his sister to university in Beijing. Simultaneously his country was rapidly changing as China opened up to the Western world and to capitalism. Suddenly, thousands of young Chinese students were leaving their country to study abroad for the first time in several decades. Nonetheless, when Junjie arrived in London he was the only student in his

FIG 5.2 Junjie's family watching TV in Dong Xiao Wu

programme who had never been outside his home country before. His university courses had included classes on the thoughts of Mao and on Marxism. Suddenly, he was surrounded by young people who had been almost everywhere, spoke several languages, shared a more or less similar Western educational background and had all been watching 'Friends' on television, not reading the works of Mao. The first months in London were overwhelming for Junjie, who struggled with English, with new university courses, and with his new way of life.

FIG 5.3 Shani imitating a pop star as a teenager when visiting Kinneret

However, Junjie's departure, like Shani's and Terhi's, was not as dramatic as that of Shani's grandfather from Latvia: they do go back, and they can communicate on a regular basis with family at home. Only since the 1970s have Finnish and Israeli families encountered globalization through all scapes. It is only since that time that these societies have faced full-scale globalization. This is what Junjie's generation faces now in China.

Shani and Junjie are not as place bound at the moment as Terhi eventually turned out to be. They are more than 20 years younger than she and have not yet settled down. They keep their options open and could choose to go anywhere. However, Shani says that when she has children she wants to go back to Israel. She has an Israeli husband, feeling that in the present political situation nobody else can understand the anxieties she goes through. She speaks Hebrew with her husband at home. Junjie spent much of his leisure time in London with other Chinese students and was able to speak his own language with them. Shani and Junjie have both de-territorialized their cultures, mainly by bringing their languages with them.

Shani and Junjie have left their home countries, at least temporarily, and become globalized if not cosmopolitanized. Another way of analysing heterogenization is to look at the youngest members of the Finnish family. Unlike Shani and Junjie, they do not have access to globalization through studying abroad or in any of the other ways that are often considered privileged. They are young people who had been struggling with

FIG 5.4 Nyrki watching TV with his friends in Helsinki

unemployment, with basic education but no professional skills. They have also been exposed to global media more than any other members of the families in this study. Nyrki and Sampo emblemize the MTV generation, which grew up surrounded by global culture without moving.

Despite being members of the global MTV generation, Nyrki and Sampo also listen to Finnish music. In their tastes for music, they are not alone: if one looks at any statistics of records sold in Finland, Finnish music still sells at least as well as foreign music. Where they are different from many Finns of their age is in their interest in black music: Sampo has even written lyrics to rap music distributed by a small underground company and thus contributed to the indigenization of rap in an almost mono-cultural society. His 11-year-old sister listens to Finnish children's rap presented by a young Finnish artist. Rap music in Finland is a classic example of transculturation as defined by Lull (see earlier), 'whereby cultural forms literally move through time and space where they interact with other cultural forms and settings, influence each other, produce new forms, change cultural settings and produce cultural hybrids' (2000: 242–3).

The taste in films of the youngest generation of the Finnish family also reflects the combination of national and global. Nyrki's favourite films include *Scarface* (USA), *Pulp Fiction* (USA), *Boyz in the Hood* (USA), *La Haine*

FIG 5.5 Nyrki listening to a Walkman in Heidelberg

(France) and the films of Finnish film director Aki Kaurismaki (*Leningrad Cowboys Go to America, The Man without a Past*). As children and teenagers, Nyrki and his brother Sampo watched on television 'Knight Rider', 'McGyver', 'Dallas', 'Twin Peaks', and 'Beverly Hills', but also Finnish shows such as 'Pultti-Boys' or 'Hymyhuulet'. Nyrki's tastes in both films and television programme are again not exceptional in Finland; foreign films are popular, but increasingly Finnish films have also gained huge popularity.

Nyrki, and especially his younger brother Sampo, also became interested in computer games early on. They got their first video game in Ceuta (a Spanish enclave in North Africa) while holidaying in Spain in the early 1980s. It was a first-generation football video game, and was followed by many other sports and adventure games. They got their first computer, an Atari, in the late 1980s when they started playing computer games such as Kick Off, Sim City and NHL Hockey. Computer games separate them completely from previous generations, who have never played them, although both Terhi and Eila use computers for work.

The same concerns mobile phones (the word for a mobile phone in Finnish is *känny*, a diminutive form of 'hand'). In Finland there are 76.5 mobile phones per 100 inhabitants,[2] and young people often started using them earlier than their parents. Sending and receiving of text messages have become essential functions among the users of mobile phones. Young people, especially young women, send a lot of text messages, whereas the older age groups use them less frequently. A total of one billion text messages, or close on 300 per mobile phone user, were sent in Finland in the year 2000.[3] Rheingold has observed young people's behaviour in Helsinki:

> I watched five Finns meet and talk on the sidewalk. Three were in their early twenties. Two were old enough to be the younger people's parents. One of the younger persons looked down at his mobile phone while he was talking to one of the older people. The young man smiled and then showed the screen of his telephone to his peers, who looked at each other and smiled. However, the young man holding his device didn't show his mobile phone's screen to the older two. The sidewalk conversation among the five people flowed smoothly, apparently unperturbed by the activities I witnessed. Whatever the young three were doing, it was clearly part of an accepted social code I knew nothing about. A new mode of social communication, enabled by new technology, had already diffused into the norms of Finnish society. (2002: xvi)

The picture Rheingold is painting is a familiar sight in urban life in Finland, where mobile phones have become a part of everyday culture and communication. Younger people use mobile phones more distinctively than adults to form their own social networks, where they combine oral and written communication by texting messages to each other, as Figure 5.6 shows.

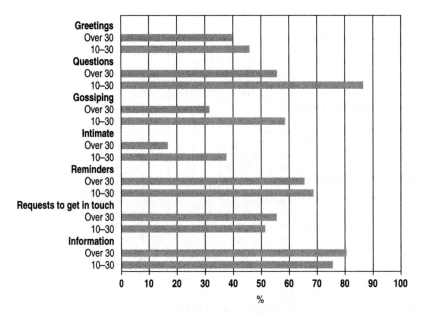

FIG 5.6 Content of text messages sent by persons under 30 years, November 1999 (per cent)

Source: Statistics Finland, 'Mobile phones and computers as parts of everyday life in Finland'[4]

What we see are new forms of communication emerging that are both face-to-face and mediated interaction at the same time (see Chapter 1). Mäenpää (2001: 109) concludes that the mobile enables real-time control over the modern, dispersed and non-local networks of human relationships. This even has implications beyond the locality. He writes:

> It gives its 'user' a sense of 'where it's at', which is analogous with the 'global village' united by the media. The inhabitants of the 'global village' routinely and repeatedly update their knowledge of current affairs, for example by watching the evening news every night. The real-time network maintained by the mobile can be regarded as an intimate equivalent of living in the flux of public mass media information. The mobile phone does not convey news of the world but information on the lives of friends and acquaintances. From media culture's point of view it offers a personal, custom-made 'reality-TV'. (2001: 109)

Nyrki and Sampo are, like their peers, also much more skilful than their parents and grandparents in text messaging, thus returning to a script medium (see Chapter 3) but combining it with the latest technology. Mobile phones have already replaced phone calls and even letters, as we can see from Figure 5.7.

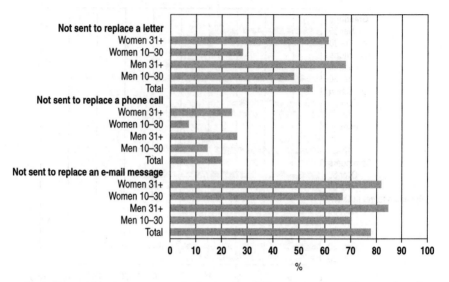

FIG 5.7 Users of text messages who had not sent them to replace other modes of communication, by age and gender, 1999 (per cent)

Source: Statistics Finland, 'Mobile phones and computers as parts of everyday life in Finland'[5]

CONCLUSION

As shown in Chapters 3 and 4, the consequence of globalization is neither homogenization nor heterogenization, but both of these, either simultaneously or sequentially. We need a much more detailed analysis in order to understand the consequences of globalization. There is no point in arguing about whether it is a process of homogenization or one of heterogenization; we need to acknowledge that it can be both and that they are not mutually exclusive. Both are present in the process of globalization and should be accepted as primary outcomes of globalization. We need to know more about the circumstances that produce either of the outcomes.

The heterogenization school has clearly failed to give enough attention to the homogenizing elements of globalization. It is difficult to deny the power that Western global media companies currently exercise. When we look at our three families, we can see that the youngest generation – and to a certain extent the previous generations – have been heavily influenced by Anglo-American media. It would also be a mistake to say that this influence is not inevitably accompanied by capitalism, to which most countries of the world have been exposed since the collapse of communism.

However, the members of these families cannot be seen only as victims of evil capitalist global media. They have been connected, through these media and forms of communication, in their similarities, but they have also remained unconnected in their differences. Clearly, the youngest generation is the most connected generation and able to share many symbols carried by Western media. They remain different from each other because of their differences in religion, ideology, upbringing, language and interests. The youngest generation is by any standard the most connected generation of the three families. No generation has ever before had as much access to media and communications as they do.

The families are also separated from each other in their access. The separation is partly societal, partly individual. It is clear that access to globalization is dependent on resources available to societies and individuals. There are billions of families in the world whose access to media and communications is not even close to that of our three families. Globalization is, without doubt, a very uneven process, which brings much misery into people's lives, either because they are excluded from it or because they are part of it.

The Finnish family is a good example of the process. The great-grandparents of the family suffered many hardships of which the younger generations have no idea. Finland was considered one of the poorest countries in the world in the nineteenth and early twentieth century. It has also been described as the most Americanized country in Europe in the late twentieth century, because of its massive importing of US cultural goods and ideas. Quite surprisingly, in the twenty-first century it is considered by the World Economic Forum to be the leading information society in the world, followed by the USA, Singapore and Sweden.[6] There is no reason to idealize Finland, since the distribution of wealth has become more and more polarized as a consequence of a partial demolition of the welfare society, but the country offers an example of a change for the better, which was once considered unthinkable. This has meant that even those who are unemployed have some kind of access to the information society, because of skills and public resources (such as libraries to which they have access). As Castells and Himanen (2001: 20) have remarked, of the three information societies (Finland, the USA and Singapore) which they analysed, Finland comes closest to an open model of the information society. This is also a form of indigenization: the heavy influence of Americanization has led to a hybridized, but also distinctively separate, model which has proved itself in some ways stronger even than the original.

NOTES

1 http://www.morim.com/hebrew_us.htm, 3 March 2003.
2 http://www.stat.fi/tk/yr/tietoyhteiskunta/matkapuhelin_vrteurooppa_kuvasivu_en.html, 2 August 2003
3 http://www.stat.fi/tk/yr/tietoyhteiskunta/matkapuhelin_en.html, 2 August 2003.

4 http://www.stat.fi/tk/yr/tietoyhteiskunta/matkapuhelin_tekstiviestisisalto_
   kuvasivu_en.html#tekstiviestisisalto, 2 August 2003.
5 http://www.stat.fi/tk/yr/tietoyhteiskunta/matkapuhelin_tekstiviestisisalto_
   kuvasivu_en.html#tekstiviestisisalto, 2 August 2003.
6 http://www.nelonen.fi/fi/talous/33346/, 3 March 2003.

6 MEDIATED COSMOPOLITANISM?

Kalliolle, kukkulalle rakennan minä majani.
Tule, tule tyttö nuori jakamaan se mun kanssani,
Jos en minä sinua saa, lähden täältä kauas pois,
Muille maille vierahille jotten sua nähdä vois.

(On the rock, in the field, I will build my house.
Come, sweet girl, to live with me,
If you don't like me then I will leave the realm,
To other foreign strands where I won't see you anymore.)

Traditional Finnish folk song (Virtanen and Dubois, 2000: 169)

Over the last decade, several scholars (see, for example, Hannerz, 1990; Tomlinson, 1999; Beck, 2000a; 2000b) in many fields have asked whether it is possible for people to become cosmopolitans. The word 'cosmopolitan' comes from two Greek words, *cosmos* and *polis*. *Cosmos* means the universe, especially as a well-ordered whole, but also an ordered system of ideas and a total experience (*Oxford Modern English Dictionary*, 1992). *Polis* means a city, and hence a state. 'Cosmopolis' is thus literally a world city, although this sense does not exist in Greek. The word *polités* means a citizen, and a cosmopolitan has thus come to mean a citizen of the world, that is, one who regards or treats the whole world as her/his country, one who has no national attachments or prejudices (*Oxford English Dictionary*, 1989). Dictionaries endow the word 'cosmopolitan' with further connotations, such as 'having an exciting and glamorous character associated with travel and mixture of cultures' (*Concise Oxford Dictionary*, 1999) or being 'broad-minded, catholic, open-minded, urbane, well-travelled and worldly-wise' (*Collins Compact Dictionary and Thesaurus*, 2001).

However, academics have, at least partly, different connotations in mind. Cosmopolitanism was previously defined as an individual, rather than a mass, project. Lie and Servaes (2000: 18) observe that cosmopolitanism seems to be a quality of individual human beings, far more than a group process or a group quality. Now academics are discussing whether cosmopolitanism could become a mass movement. Previously defined as going beyond the national, cosmopolitanism is now defined as going beyond the local. In a recent academic context cosmopolitanism has been defined as a 'home-plus' experience, as something beyond one's local experience (Hannerz, 1990: 238).

As Hannerz (1990: 237) writes, there are two ways to relate to the globalization process: that which is characteristic of cosmopolitans, and that which is characteristic of locals. Tomlinson also defines cosmopolitanism in relation to the local, for him it is 'to be able to live in both the global and the local at the same time' (1999: 167). Tomlinson's view comes close to that of Beck (2000a: 72–3), who speaks of place polygamy – access to several places at the same time. Beck gives the example of a German woman who divided her time between two places, one in Germany and one in Kenya.

However, one could argue that perhaps having access to two places, even if they are in two different countries and continents, does not necessarily in itself make one a cosmopolitan. Even if it does, such access is possible only for very few people. For most people, leaving one's place still means a much more drastic change, and access to two places is rarely as nicely balanced as it was in the life of the said German woman. As Robbins and Cheah (1998: 3) argue, rather than an ideal of detachment, actual existing cosmopolitanism is a reality of (re)attachment, multiple attachment, or attachment at a distance. Robbins and Cheah's concept of attachment at a distance again brings media and communications into the picture: how can we be attached at a distance, if not by media and communications?

The shift in definition raises another issue: the definition of the local. There is a tendency in the scholarly literature to see localities in a Heideggerian way: as something unspoilt and pure, where experience is non-mediated, based on personal communication, and democratic. In many of the definitions of localities, especially those of Heidegger or Relph, media and communications are not a component of 'genuine' places, but rather represent a threat to them, a kind of 'placelessness'. However, localities can also be seen as ever changing environments which are open to external influences. Beck (2000a: 20) raises this point, arguing that in developed modernity there is no 'natural' community of neighbours, family or nation; there are only myths of 'naturalness'. As noted in earlier chapters, even localities have become 'glocalized' (Robertson, 1995; 50), again largely because of media and communications. This also implies that there is a possibility of attaining cosmopolitanism even while staying in one place.

Cosmopolitanism is thus closely linked to globalization and the reactions it provokes. It can be seen as one of the responses to globalization, but admittedly just one of the many I have mentioned. The discussion around cosmopolitanism touches many arenas of globalization, but above all that of individual attitudes and reactions to globalization.

Cosmopolitanism is often viewed, in both academic and non-academic literature, as a kind of awareness or attitude. For Hannerz (1990: 238) cosmopolitanism is a perspective, a state of mind, or a mode of managing meaning, and cosmopolitans are those who have a willingness to engage with the other. Cosmopolitanism has also been defined as a skill which has to be acquired. For Hannerz, 'cosmopolitanism is a matter of competence . . . of both a generalized and a more specialized kind' (1990: 293). He writes:

> There is the aspect of a state of readiness, a personal ability to make one's way into other cultures, through listening, looking, intuiting and reflecting. And there is cultural competence in the stricter sense of the term, a built-up skill in manoeuvring more or less expertly with a particular system of meanings and meaningful forms. (1990: 293)

Hannerz refers to media and communications when he writes that 'the implosive power of the media may now make just about everybody a little more cosmopolitan' (1990: 249). For Tomlinson (1999: 194), a cosmopolitan needs: (1) an active sense of belonging to the wider world, of being able to experience a 'distanciated identity'; (2) a reflexive awareness of the world as one of many cultural others; (3) an ongoing dialogue; and (4) to be able to live at the same time in both the global and the local. Although Tomlinson does not refer directly to media and communications, the various options he poses – at least the first two – do leave space for them.

Hannerz suggests that cosmopolitanism can be achieved through listening, looking, intuiting and reflecting. Both non-academic and academic literature in general suggest either explicitly or indirectly that this competence may be acquired mainly through travelling: in other words, that leaving one's place physically and increasing face-to-face communication are the only ways to achieve a cosmopolitan attitude.

However, even travelling has been defined rather narrowly. According to Hannerz (1990: 241; see also Tomlinson, 1999: 185), true cosmopolitans are different from other globally mobile people – tourists, exiles, expatriates, transnational employees, migrant workers. Hannerz thus excludes the overwhelming majority of ordinary people who are currently on the move. In 2002, according to the United Nations, at least 185 million people worldwide were living outside their countries of birth, as compared with 80 million three decades earlier. For example, in 1999, 23.6 per cent of Australia's resident population was foreign born. This was higher than in Canada (17.4 per cent, according to the 1996 census), Sweden (11.8 per cent), the United States (10.3 per cent), the Netherlands (9.8 per cent) and Norway (6.5 per cent). It is estimated that 21.7 million people – or almost one out of every 275 people on earth – are refugees, returned refugees or internally displaced persons.[1]

These people do not fit into a definition of a (male) cosmopolitan, someone more like Jules Verne's nineteenth-century hero Phileas Fogg, who travelled around the world in 80 days and then returned to his Reform Club in London with a foreign wife rescued from her own culture. Fogg, however, apparently did not achieve the higher consciousness of a cosmopolitan, although he did perhaps achieve an understanding of how to live in an intercultural marriage. Verne concludes his book:

But what then? What had he really gained by all this trouble? What had he brought back from this long and weary journey?
Nothing, say you? Perhaps so; nothing but a charming woman, who, strange as it may appear, made him the happiest of men!
Truly, would you not for less than that make the tour around the world?[2]

It was up to Aouda, Fogg's Indian wife, to adjust to life in a country not her own, where she would be referred to for the rest of her life as the 'exotic' Indian wife of Mr Phileas Fogg. Of the two, she probably developed far more cosmopolitan qualities than her husband, because they would be constantly required and tested in her everyday life.

It is not surprising that, when cosmopolitanism is defined in an elistist way, there is little scope for ordinary people to achieve cosmopolitan qualities. The concept has, indeed, been criticized for its elitism. Tomlinson (1999: 187–8) summed up the criticisms levelled at the concept, referring to its sexist and Western take on things. According to Tomlinson, it is clearly a Western view of the *homme du monde* as opposed to the *mujer en la casa*, where the man conquers the world and the woman stays at home. He quotes Massey (1994: 165) who has pointed out that cosmopolitanism is a predominantly white and First World take on things, involving the denigration of locally situated cultural experience, or at least its subordination to the practice of 'higher' consciousness. But if this is the case, does this mean that ordinary people have no opportunities to become cosmopolitans? Can somebody become a cosmopolitan not by changing places but through media and communications?

If this is possible, what also interests me, as a media and communications scholar, is whether it is possible to have a mass movement of cosmopolitans. As Beck puts it, in a play on Marx's famous phrase, 'Cosmopolitans of the world, unite!' (2000b: 176). Inevitably, this means that we need to ask whether cosmopolitanism can be mediated. The possible mediation of cosmopolitanism leads us to a second question: whether cosmopolitanism can be mass-mediated.

Again, as so many times before, globalization scholars have left aside the role of media and communications. Beck, however, acknowledges it indirectly when he writes that 'cosmopolitanism is the question of level of mediation' (2000b: 176). Again, of course, for most of those people who do not travel as tourists or leave their countries at all, media and communications provide their main channel to other parts of the world. What we know about the war in Afghanistan or the presidential election in Zimbabwe is almost exclusively based on the information we receive from the media, if we are not directly or indirectly involved. The possibility of cosmopolitanism draws heavily on access, be it physical or visual. As Bauman (2001) has observed, television provides artificial eyes, but no arms. He writes:

FIG 6.1 Tyyne and Sisko travelling near Athens

> But while our hands have not grown any longer, we have acquired 'artificial eyes' which enable us to see what our eyes never would. The challenges to our moral conscience exceed many times over that conscience's ability to cope and stand up to challenge. To restore the lost moral balance, we would need 'artificial hands' stretching as far as our artificial eyes are able to.

This leads to the most fundamental question about cosmopolitanism: what does it mean to be able to see, but not reach? Although in our global society it is impossible to avoid neighbours, what are we to do when we see that our neighbours are 'bad', for example, that they violate human rights? What if we become aware of this, but lack the 'arms' to change it?

ZONES OF COSMOPOLITANISM

Unlike the theorists I have quoted, I argue that individuals cannot become complete cosmopolitans, just as they cannot become complete Finns,

Chinese or Israelis, for example. Cosmopolitan identity is like any other identity and is not an overall identity that excludes every other identity. Instead of considering how individuals could become cosmopolitans, I would suggest that people can develop cosmopolitan qualities, a cosmopolitan identity. One way to understand this process is to suggest that there are different 'zones' within cosmopolitanism. These should not be understood as exclusive, or as constituting a step-by-step programme for reaching the highest level. What I am suggesting, though, is that none of these zones is sufficient in itself, and that one probably needs to occupy more than one 'zone' to achieve cosmopolitan qualities. Even somebody who has visited all the zones is unlikely to be completely and permanently above nationalist or local sentiments; I consider that to be unrealistic. After all, cosmopolitanism is a state of mind which can easily be swept away in special circumstances such as international political crises or terrorist attacks, as we see repeatedly when war breaks out somewhere in the world. Both nationalism and cosmopolitanism are not rational projects, but instead very emotional projects. Nationalism-free zones may exist, as well as cosmopolitanism-free zones. All zones are linked to one other either by personal contacts or by mediated communication.

There is also the 'safety zone' that allows each of us to go back to what is most familiar to us. Relph (1976: 10) writes about perceptual space – the egocentric space perceived and confronted by each individual where action is centred on immediate needs and practices. One's native language is the best example: even the most multilingual people feel capable of expressing their deepest feelings only in their first language. This can also be described as 'going home' or 'closing the door' wherever that home or that door is, or it may mean taking one's home with one, living, for example, in one of those many Chinatowns around the world, in a Little Italy (like London's Clerkenwell) or a Little Russia (like New York's Brighton Beach).

I aim to look beyond the traditional, individual (male) explorer's definition of cosmopolitanism, and to extend the concept into the possibility of everyday cosmopolitanism, whilst bearing in mind that cosmopolitanism is not something fixed and stable, but something that is on the move. I suggest that there are five zones of everyday cosmopolitanism:

1   media and communications
2   learning another language
3   living/working abroad or having a family member living abroad
4   living with a person from another culture
5   engaging with foreigners in your locality or across a frontier.

Media and Communications

Even in the most geographically and culturally remote places, where no foreigners are ever encountered, the media can provide access to the world outside one's own place. This is, of course, one-way mass communication when it happens through the media, to quote Bauman, enabling the eyes and ears, but not the voice to talk back. In the case of communications this may be an interpersonal and two-way process, but it still lacks the physical contact and support that face-to-face communication gains from non-verbal communication. However, the influence of media and communications cannot be denied. For many people in the world, it is the only way they can reach the outer world beyond their own location. A counter-argument can be made that comparatively few people have access to media and communications. Still, simple numbers show the growth of media and communications around the world, in developing as well as in developed countries, with more and more people gaining access to them.

Media is about connecting strangers to one other, whether or not they have expressed their willingness. In this sense, when the 'neighbourhood' is the world, refusing to hear or see the neighbours is not an option. This is why the first images of the famine in Biafra in the early 1970s were so powerful: few people in the developed world had previously seen with their own eyes children dying of hunger.

In this case, and in many others, the very fact of seeing led to action, when people started giving money to help the victims of famine. Although now, in the mature age of television, people are more and more accustomed to images of famine, natural disasters, war, terrorism and destruction, they still often react and try to do something to help. The media can connect strangers in mourning an individual, as happened when Princess Diana died in 1997, when 2.5 billion people watched her funeral and were emotionally touched by the life of a woman they could identify with despite differences of class, race, nationality and wealth. The media also connect people in the context of sports, when billions of people support individuals or teams from countries they have never been to, if their home countries do not have teams of their own. They can also connect people in the context of entertainment, with televised concerts of superstars who appeal to billions of people, despite their differences. In many ways, Tomlinson's ongoing dialogue of being able to live in both the global and the local at the same time becomes possible through media and communications, even for people who remain in one place.

Of course, the media can have exactly the opposite effect: rather than cosmopolitanism, they can promote nationalism, xenophobia and bigotry, as has happened so many times. Even if this does not happen, it would make no sense to argue that access to media is enough to make somebody a cosmopolitan, or indeed to make them anything else. It is, however, important to acknowledge the power of the media, together with other factors, to bring this about. The media can offer the global ingredients for the development of cosmopolitan awareness, but it is up to people what they make of these ingredients.

Media, and especially communications, are also present in other zones where they are the means of mediation either within one zone or between different zones.

Learning another Language

Can a person who only knows one language acquire cosmopolitan qualities? Can we fully engage with others if we do not share a language with them? Is knowledge of English enough to achieve a cosmopolitan identity? If this is the case, is every English speaker cosmopolitan? Hardly. As Edwards Raleigh wrote as early as 1868: 'He was no cosmopolitan. He was an Englishman of the English' (*Oxford English Dictionary*, 1989).[3]

In today's world, however, it would be difficult to argue that one can become cosmopolitan without any knowledge of English. This is because English has become, whether we like it or not, a working language of politics, business, culture and tourism. By 1995, 75 countries had officially recognized English as a primary or a secondary language. The number of people who speak English as a first or second language has been estimated at approximately 573 million, a quarter of the world's population (Short and Kim, 1999: 78). Three-quarters of the world's mail is written in English. About 80 per cent of the world's electronically stored information is in English (Skapinger, 2000). This has resulted in the increase of the number of people who can speak English as their second language. For example, more than half of continental Europeans can speak at least one foreign language (some 41 per cent of them speak English) and sometimes even two. Almost 80 per cent of Swedish, Danish and Dutch people can speak English. At the same time, 66 per cent of the British population have absolutely no knowledge of any other language than English (Osborn, 2001).

There are also countries that are multilingual (for example, Finland with 2 official languages, Switzerland with 4, India with 18), but that does not make their citizens necessarily more cosmopolitan than others. Indeed, people can become trapped in defending their own language against another, as happens in many bilingual communities. Interestingly, for example, a French-speaking Quebecois student studying outside Quebec finds him/herself speaking English with other non-native English speakers, for all of whom it is the second language. To take another example, Nordic people, who are commonly supposed to speak a mutually understandable 'Skandinaviska', in practice have difficulties doing so, and speak English instead, finding it, as a second language for all of them, more democratic. Then there is the case of Latvians, Lithuanians and Estonians, who all understand Russian, which was until recently the compulsory official language in all three countries, but now choose to communicate with each other in English, which comes without historical and political baggage.

As a result of the spread of English, it is spoken in a variety of ways, often quite remote from the 'Queen's English'. Linguistics has had to acknowledge this, and the concept of one official grammar shared by many has been superseded. Linguistics now divides English speakers into three groups (Skapinger, 2000). The first group consists of people for whom English is the first and often only language. They live in their largest numbers in the US, the UK, Canada, Australia, New Zealand, Ireland and Jamaica. The second group consists of people who speak English as their second language; they live in countries (often former colonies) where English has a special status, such as India, Nigeria, Singapore and the Philippines. The third group consists of the growing number of people learning English as a foreign language in countries with no strong US or British connections. As a result, English is spoken in a variety of ways and it is no longer the exclusive property of Britain or the US (Skapinger, 2000). This is the de-territorialization of English.

With English more widely spoken, there is now a quest for other languages. Multi-national companies are increasingly looking for people with the ability to speak at least two languages. Knowing English only makes sense if it is combined with other languages, since the knowledge of those languages gives access to other cultures and an ability to move from one culture to another. This is also why knowledge only of English is not enough to make someone a cosmopolitan, although certainly, since it is so widely spoken, it is easier for native English speakers to travel than for any other people. The access provided by one language does not make someone more of a cosmopolitan than watching television with subtitles or voiceover. A language is a medium which may be used or not used, just like any other medium. However, to use a language which is not one's own is to enter unknown territory, leaving one's safety zone.

When Someone in Your Family Lives or Works Abroad

Having someone in your family who lives or works abroad is one of the most common ways of becoming more cosmopolitan, even whilst staying in one place. This is the experience of millions of families around the world with members who are migrant workers. For example, over the past 20 years, Britain has experienced a total net inflow of 1.2 million people. Each year about 100,000 more people remain in Britain than leave. In Britain, one in three doctors, one in 10 nurses, 13 per cent of teachers and researchers in universities, and 70 per cent of catering workers are foreign.[4]

All these people have left behind family members and friends with whom they remain in contact. As a result, the experience affects not only migrant workers themselves, but also their families. The economic importance of international migration also plays a determining role for their families at home. For some countries, the funds sent home by migrants represent a significant source of foreign exchange earnings. For example, in 2000 India received remittances of $11.6bn, Mexico $6.6bn, Turkey $54.6bn and Egypt $53.7bn. If one ranks the 20 largest recipients of remittances by the ratio of their receipts to gross domestic product, Jordan comes top with 21.8 per cent of GDP, followed by Yemen with 13.6 per cent, El Salvador with 13.3 per cent and Jamaica with 10.7 per cent (*Financial Times*, 2003).[5]

The experience of immigration also changes their families in other ways. Those who leave to work abroad are changed by the experience, and bring back their experiences and knowledge (be it a new language or new customs) to their home communities. A letter or a videotape sent home from abroad tells of previously unknown countries. An economic or political refugee may become a permanent exile, remaining abroad even when the necessity is past. Families become more and more globalized whether they want to or not as their members settle in different countries.

Living with a Person from Another Culture

The definition of cosmopolitanism has largely excluded women. This is because, as Tomlinson puts it, *mujeres en la casa* are supposed to stay at home while men go out and conquer the world. This may still be true, especially

FIG 6.2 Junjie's graduation ceremony in Los Angeles

in certain professions such as business or the military. However, there is one 'profession' where women's experience has been more global than men's: that of leaving their countries to marry and become *mujeres en la casa* in another country. For example, in 1960 nearly everyone who married in the Federal Republic was German. By 1994, however, the man or the woman or both were foreign citizens in one out of every seven marriage ceremonies (Beck-Gernsheim, 2002: 124). The women who have married globally have created new homes away from their home countries and thus combined at least two cultures. This has had an effect not only on their spouses, but also on their children growing up in multi-cultural families. These women are active in running their own informal support networks, local language schools, churches, magazines etc. They also keep in contact with friends and families in their home countries by writing, sending packages, calling, e-mailing and visiting them regularly. They bring their cooking and decorating style into their new homes and try to combine it with their spouses' local taste. The result is often a mixture of two cultures or a hybridized local culture, but it is never entirely the same as it was before. Their children, although often abandoning their mother's tongue, become citizens of their father's country, but always with a touch of 'otherness'.

Mujeres en la casa are also on the move. Increasingly, in monolingual and mono-cultural families, where women work outside the home, domestic workers are hired to look after the children or do the household work. For example, about 1.5 million Asian women, both legal and illegal, are working abroad, with a large proportion of them in other Asian countries – the Gulf countries and the fast-growing Asian economies of the East. In Spain, domestic work is the largest single area of female employment, while in France more than 50 per cent of migrant women are employed in domestic work. In Italy, there are 1.2 million female domestic workers, of whom only 18 per cent are legally employed. Approximately half of the total are foreign workers. In 1995, a third of work permits issued were given to domestic workers.[6] Again, these women, although their status is different to that of the spouses, bring their own language, accent, style and cooking, but need to meet their employers' expectations.

Engaging with Other Cultures in Your Locality

Engaging with foreigners does not necessarily include leaving one's own place. As many authors have shown, there are cities, such as London or New York, where a whole world is accessible. In London, 300 languages are spoken. It has been described as a city 'where you can order breakfast in Farsi, book a taxi in Urdu, ask for afternoon coffee in Arabic, and spend the evening chatting with your friends in Cantonese'[7]. It is possible to move from one 'country' to another without leaving London, just by moving from one neighbourhood into another.

Castells (1993: 326–30) introduces the concept of the informational (global) city with a polarized occupational structure in which elitist cosmopolitans live with a daily connection to the whole world, in contrast to the tribalism of local communities. According to him, the fundamental dividing line in our cities is between the inclusion of cosmopolitans in the making of the new history, and the exclusion of locals from control of the global city to which their neighbourhoods ultimately belong. This is, of course, a danger even in global cities. However, I would argue that it fails to take account of the possibility of interaction and the nature of diasporic communities. I would even argue that Castell's 'cosmopolitans', living in their non-places, probably live a less cosmopolitan life than those who encounter differences and conflicts between various cultures while still living in their place of origin.

As Georgiou (2001: 322) has shown, diasporic groups use media and communications not only to connect with their former home countries. Increasingly, especially for the younger generations, there is a combination of the old and the new: they have access to many cultures, which are becoming more independent of place. Diasporic media scholars now argue for different hybrid forms of culture emerging through mediated and unmediated access. The older generation has its memories from the former home country, but lives in a new country; while the younger generation's only memories are from its present country, but they are connected to their parents' former home countries through their parents and through media and communications. However, during this process the image of their homeland has already become partly illusory.

There is no longer either the culture of the country of origin or that of the country of residence, but a third culture that has elements from both but has already become something different. Thus, in principle, one can experience all these cultures while living in one city.

FOUR FAMILY TREES: WHO TALKS TO WHOM?

Thinking of the four generations of our three families, we need to ask: (1) who has had the opportunity to achieve cosmopolitan qualities; and (2) who has had the desire to achieve them? If we define cosmopolitanism as it has traditionally been defined, the Latvian great-grandfather Moshe, with his knowledge of several languages and of travel, was the first with potential cosmopolitan qualities. He remained in place and did not leave. His son Lasik, who did leave his original home country, rather than becoming an advocate for cosmopolitanism became a strong advocate of Israeli patriotism. The Chinese great–grandfather Baosheng, at the same time, was bound to his home village with no access to media and communications. He could not choose and remained what he was: a man embedded in his locality without an early articulated affiliation to his home country. The Finnish great-grandmother Tyyne when young was no different from the Chinese great-grandfather Baosheng, their primary affiliation being with the place where they were born. The Chinese and Finnish great-grandparents all later developed a sense of nationalism towards the territory they identified, beyond their own place, as their home country.

FIG 6.3 Sisko and Eila celebrating Eila's 70th birthday in Pécs

TABLE 6.1 Family 1: cosmopolitan

	Great-grandmother Tyyne, 1905–87	Grandmother Eila, 1927–	Mother Terhi, 1953–	Son Nyrki, 1976–
Languages spoken	Finnish	Finish, Swedish, German, English	Finnish, English, Swedish, Russian	Finnish, English
First overseas journey	At age 63 to Norway	At age 20 to Sweden	At age 10 to Sweden	At age 3 to Sweden
Travel	Nordic countries, Europe, USA	Nordic countries, Europe, N. America, S. America, Australia, Africa	Nordic countries, Europe, N. America, Asia, Australia, Africa	Nordic countries, Europe, N. America, Asia, Australia
Interests	Knitting, reading, gardening, religion	Reading, radio and television gardening, classical music, theatre, golf	Reading, exercise, music (pop and classical), movies, gardening	Black music (soul, funk), television, videos, reading, football

Unlike the Chinese great-grandfather Baosheng, who lacked the access to and the means of travel, the Finnish great-grandmother Tyyne became a keen traveller in her sixties when she could afford it with the help of her daughters: she loved travelling abroad and was deeply interested in the countries she visited, although she did not speak any foreign languages (Table 6.1). According to her Christian faith, everybody was equal before God. Her daughters, Eila and Sisko, had access through education, through their knowledge of languages, through their willingness to work and travel abroad to other cosmopolitan zones. Eila opted, in the end, for the local: she now lives in her original home town where her parents lived.

This is also what happened to the Israeli father: after years of extensive travelling and working abroad he now lives back in his home country. The Israeli and Finnish families both experienced war: the Israeli family is currently in the midst of war, and Eila in Finland, still remembers how her home town of Kotka was bombed in 1939–44 and how she and her family hid in a cellar. The Chinese great-grandfather Baosheng and grandfather Zhansheng also have such memories of war. It made them all nationalistic, giving them a feeling that they belonged to something larger, beyond their own localities (Table 6.3). The Israeli daughter Shani in London struggles with her feelings: there are times, for example when her brother was enlisted in the Israeli army, when she finds it very difficult not to be emotionally involved and to maintain her cosmopolitanism (Table 6.4).

TABLE 6.2 Sisko's (born in 1930) travels

Year	Location	Year	Location
1944	Sweden	1986	Hungary, Spain
1963	Sweden	1987	Iceland
1964	Spain	1988	Sweden, Spain
1965	Sweden and Norway	1989	Austria, Egypt, Germany, USA
1970	Denmark	1990	UK, Greece
1972	Austria, Hungary	1991	Norway, Germany, Sweden,
1973	France, the Netherlands		Portugal
1973	Spain	1992	Hungary, Spain, Hungary-Poland-
1974	Italy		Austria, Greece
1975	Greece	1993	Iceland, Bulgaria, Greece, Spain
1976	Spain	1994	Canada, USA, UK
1977	UK	1995	Spain (twice)
1978	Greece	1996	Poland, Switzerland, Austria,
1979	Austria, Sweden		Spain
1980	Rumania	1997	the Netherlands, Greenland,
1981	Spain		Hungary, China, Greece
1982	UK	1998	Germany, Poland, Italy, Spain
1983	Malta		(twice)
1984	Austria, Germany, Luxembourg,	1999	UK, Spain, the Czech Republic,
	Switzerland		Estonia
1985	China, Hong Kong, Japan,		
	Portugal, Madeira		

TABLE 6.3 Family 2: Cosmopolitanism

	Great-grandfather Baosheng, 1888–1971	Grandfather Zhansheng, 1923–2000	Father Qinghe 1944–	Son Junjie 1974–
Languages spoken	Chinese Dialect	Chinese Dialect	Chinese Dialect	Chinese Dialect, Mandarin, English
First overseas journey	Never	Never	Never	At the age of 27 to UK, then USA
Travel	Some places in China	Many places in China	Many places in China	China, UK, USA
Interests	Chinese traditional opera, books, Chinese calligraphy	Chinese traditional opera, Chinese traditional fiction books, radio, television series	Television series, television news	Chinese calligraphy, Western classical music, playing basketball, Chinese traditional fiction, books

FIG 6.4 Terhi looking for St Petersburg in Clarion County, Pennsylvania

Terhi, on the other hand, is very critical of nationalism, much more so than her mother or her children. Lo has remarked that 'identities are about attachments to, and embeddedness in, times and places. Few really qualify as footloose cosmopolitans in the narrow sense of cosmopolitanism, meaning a "non-commitment and unfeeling detachment from particular affective and concrete ties [to specific times and places] etc."' (2002: 70). Terhi is by no means footloose and is very sentimental about times and places in her former home country, but feels completely detached from Finnish national ideology when it is defined as anti-Russian, anti-Swedish or 'anti-foreignness'. This attitude was strengthened when her son Sampo was imprisoned in Finland for refusing to do his national military service.[8]

Terhi's present life in the UK, where men have not been forced to do military service for more than 40 years, has also given her a different perspective on the necessity for military service, which is almost unquestioned in Finland. Her daily life in London, as a foreigner among many other foreigners, has fundamentally changed her; whenever she goes back to Helsinki, she feels that something is missing in the mono-culturalism of her former home town. At the same time, she also feels alienated from the national ideology and strong militarism of her new home country. After 6 years she is still 'in between' the two countries and does not think of herself as a citizen of any one country.

Shani's and Junjie's positions are different, because they are not planning to stay in London. Shani has already been living in London for 5 years and feels at home there, to as great an extent as a foreigner can. For Junjie it has been more difficult. Still they all, from time to time, for many reasons, feel lost and lonely in a foreign country and need to go back to their comfort zones.

They all find these safety zones in their own languages. Junjie and Shani both had many fellow students from their home countries with whom they could talk and spend time. Terhi has no close Finnish colleagues or friends in London; she often calls her Finnish friend Paula in Exeter when she feels the need to express herself in her own language. All three call their family members frequently, several times a week, every week or two.

TABLE 6.4 Family 3: cosmopolitanism

	Great-grandfather Moshe, 1881–1941	Grandfather Lasik, 1912–97	Father Nechemya, 1941–	Daughter Shani, 1972–
Languages spoken	Russian, Yiddish, Latvian, basic Hebrew (only for prayer purposes)	Latvian, Yiddish, Russian, Hebrew	Hebrew, English basic French	Hebrew, English
First overseas journey	None	As a teenager to the Baltic countries	At age 20, leisure trip to Cyprus	At age 5, to Turkey (part of father's work commission)
Travel	None	Russia, Finland, Estonia, Lithuania (at age 20), Germany, Belgium, France (at age 60)	Kenya, Cyprus (20), South Africa (25), USA, Czechoslovakia, Ethiopia (25–34), Turkey (34), Western Europe (36)	Turkey (5), Europe (7–22), USA (23), Latin America (23)
Interests		Geography history	Flying, geography	Theatre, poetry

The media and communications in their countries of origin are an important means to feel connected and thus comforted. They all read newspapers daily on the Internet. Terhi subscribes to a Finnish women's magazine, which she reads from cover to cover, even the most trivial articles she would never have bothered to read when she lived in Finland. Junjie listened to Chinese rock when he felt homesick (which happened very rarely, he says). Food was a source of comfort for all of them. Junjie went to London's Chinatown to buy ingredients for his cooking (he cooked his own meals because he does not like British food), although he found one of the big supermarket chains almost as good. Terhi sometimes goes to the café at the Finnish Church, which also sells some 'musts' for Finnish cooking such as rye flour for baking dark bread, a rarity in London. The Finnish Guild in the UK has a chatroom on its website where the members exchange information about practical matters from buying a car to exchanging recipes.

Junjie, Shani and Terhi also use global media as a means of comfort. Junjie and Shani both watched 'Friends' and 'Sex and the City', which Terhi also watched. Junjie lived in a student dormitory where, again, he watched television with his fellow students. The 2002 football World Cup

FIG 6.5 Nyrki and Sampo playing 'Indians' in Helsinki

meant the appearance of a television set even in the student cafeteria in their university. Students from different countries all watched television together, each supporting their own favourite team. For Junjie this was Korea, the closest Asian team to reach the semi-finals. Terhi has been watching 'ER' since 1994, in Finland, in Australia and now in London. She discussed almost every episode with her British friend Carol (who now lives in France) the following day at work over a cup of tea. They were both moved by the death of Dr Green in the series, although neither of them has any difficulty in understanding the difference between fact and fiction. It was just that a character they had become used to and liked was gone.

However, it would be very wrong to conclude that only Terhi, Shani and Junjie can be defined as cosmopolitans, because they now more or less permanently live/work/study abroad. The present situation is not necessarily something that is going to last for ever. Terhi may turn into a German woman *à la* Beck who divides her time between her two countries; Shani and Junjie may go back to Israel and China and live their lives there ever after. However, their lives, like the lives of their families, have changed permanently because of their increasing awareness of what is beyond their own places and countries.

This awareness is the result of the different zones and an indication that people have become more cosmopolitan, if not cosmopolitans. The older generations were able to move beyond the local while the younger generations aspire to go beyond the national. For the first time these families are connected to each other, aware of each other in a way which was never possible before. If nationalism is something imagined, because all the members of one nation can never see each other, so is cosmopolitanism. Compared with nationalism it is still a very new idea, but it can already be seen in the everyday lives of millions of people.

CONCLUSION

Acknowledging the role of the media is an important component in the analysis of cosmopolitanism, but also a problem that needs tackling precisely because of the role of mediation. As Tomlinson (1994: 84) has pointed out, there is a difference between *mass-mediated* and *non-mass-mediated* experiences. Thompson (1995: 84) refers to the same phenomenon, using the term *mediated quasi-interaction*, whilst Harvey (1993: 14) talks of *mass-mediated social relationships*. For Harvey and Tomlinson, the problem is not only that experiences and relationships are mediated, but precisely that they are mass-mediated. Thompson goes one step further and argues that since interaction is mass-mediated, it becomes quasi. According to the *Oxford English Dictionary* (1989)[9] the prefix 'quasi' implies something which is not real, something which imitates the real ('seemingly, or in appearance, but not really; almost, nearly, virtually'). If we accept this argument, mediated cosmopolitanism is by definition a mass-mediated, and thus a false, experience.

This argument has its flaws, which go back to pre-modern times when social relationships were mainly, but not even then entirely, non-mediated. The assumption here is that when social relationships are non-mediated, they make possible an experience which is more genuine than the one that is mediated. McLuhan, in his famous coining of the term 'global village', indicates that he sees no difference in the form of social relationships when it comes to the role of media. A village denotes a relatively small entity where people know each other. The idea of the world becoming a global village refers to the physical proximity to one another of villagers.

However, Tomlinson and Thompson argue the opposite: that media and communications cannot give us the same kind of capacity for proximity as people in small communities. They both note that mediated quasi-interaction, or mass-mediated experiences, are *monological* in character, in the sense that the flow of communication is predominantly one-way (Thompson, 1995: 35–6) or lacking in dialogue (Tomlinson, 1994: 158, 168). Hence, although people live more globally through mass-mediated experience, their global and local experiences differ from each other. By their very nature, the media offer one-way experiences, which are consumed in localities by audiences, not by members of the global community (1994: 169). Tomlinson emphasizes that the consumption of television programmes is a shared experience, but not in the same way as a communal experience, because it lacks the facility for talking back.

There are several ways in which we might disagree with these writers. One possibility is to argue that their views are very similar to Tönnies's famous (1926) community–society distinction that conceptualized the change from agrarian societies to industrial societies. Thompson and Tomlinson follow the same kind of argument, but this time it is a question of moving from the national to the global, beyond the boundaries of nation-states. The idea of a community is adopted as an idea of global communication. As Tomlinson (1999: 3) writes, the idea of neighbourhood grasps something fundamental about the process of globalization: the dialectical relationship between our local lives and cultural experience, and the globalizing structures and forces that are rapidly transforming them.

This is, of course, no different from McLuhan's global village. Many of the characteristics which Tönnies used to define communities versus societies have now moved to a global level. But social relations between people change *en route,* as they did when communities became societies. Media and communications are now present almost everywhere. As Anderson (1983) reminds us, the very concept of nationhood is a concept of an imagined community. Anderson speaks of newspapers and their role in uniting citizens of the same country, most of whom never meet, through the ritual of reading newspapers, thus forming imagined communities. As Billig points out, 'the nation is to be imagined as a unique entity in terms of time and space. It is imagined as a community stretching through time, with its own past and future destiny: it is imagined across space, embracing the inhabitants of a particular territory' (1995: 70). What happens in the age of globalization is that the scale has become even larger, and what has to be imagined is the citizens of this universe.

A second point for disagreement could be the nature of media. It is difficult to argue against traditional media, since they are monological in character and predominantly one-way. However, if we include communications as well as media, the picture at once becomes different. We can include such technology as the postal service, the telegraph and the telephone, which all make it possible to talk back. They are part of globalization and have benefited from advanced means of transport and technology. All these forms are available to billions of people, although relatively developed infrastructures and skills (such as literacy) are often needed. Still, even in less developed societies, the combination of different forms of communication is visible.

With the emergence of the Internet, the clear distinction between different forms of communication (oral, script, print, electronic) partly disappears, and the Internet combines these forms: the immediacy of orality with the ability to write a message but also to 'print' it, that is to send it to an unlimited number of participants electronically. This is not necessarily monological, although it could be. It also makes it possible to switch from one role to another and back again: to be public and private, to be at the same time sender and receiver. Still, it is not difficult to argue that the Internet is only a drop in the ocean: 8 per cent of the world now has access to it. Tomlinson and Thompson make a very valid point here, and it is hard to argue against this, except with reference to the latest communications technology, which is only used by relatively few people.

There is another way to argue against the monological character of communications, but the argument must then be extended beyond both media and communications. By the 1940s, Lazarsfeld et al. (1944) had already developed the concept of a *two-step flow of communication*. They developed this concept when, while researching political campaigns, they discovered that information was passed first to opinion leaders and then from them to other people. My point here is not to suggest that this is the case with global communication (although one could argue that earlier information flowed from international to national media, from national to local media and then to its receivers), but that this division of labour is no longer necessarily entirely vertical. People are much more able to connect vertically with other people at distance than ever before.

It is equally important to realize how they are connected. They do not use only one form of media and communications, but combine them innovatively with other forms of media and communications and further with non-mass-mediated social relationships. This is necessarily no longer a two-step flow but, to use Deleuze and Guatarri's (1976) term, comprises *rhizomes* or networks of communication which combine mass and personal communication. These rhizomes, which used to be local or national, are now increasingly global. Their existence opens up the possibility of cosmopolitan identity.

NOTES

1 http://www.gcir.org/about_immigration/world_map_intro.htm, 14 February 2003.
2 http://www.literature.org/authors/verne-jules/eighty/, 14 February 2003.
3 http://athens.oed.com/cgi/entry/, 4 August 2003.
4 http://www.observer.co.uk/race/story/0,11255,856280,00.html, 14 February 2003.
5 http://portal.unesco.org/en/ev.php, 8 August 2003.
6 http://portal.unesco.org/en/ev.php@URL_ID=13200&URL_DO=DO_PRINTPAGE&URL, _SECTION=201.html, 8 August 2003.
7 http://universitiesinlondon.co.uk/student/culture.htm, 7 June 2004.
8 http://web.amnesty.org/library/index/engeur2000/2000?opendocument&of=countries, 14 February 2003.
   http://www.aseistakieltaytyjaliitto.fi/en=index.html, 14 February 2003.
9 http://athens.oed.com/cgi/entry/, 1 August 2003.

7 CONCLUSION

This book began with an idea of putting together individual life histories and some 100 years of globalization. I wanted to see not only how individual families in different locations were affected by globalization, but also how they contributed to it. I also wanted to juxtapose 'big' overarching theories with 'small' individual life histories and see whether they fitted together. Above all, I wanted to see what the role of media and communications is, both in individual lives and in globalization. The new methodology I have proposed, global mediagraphy, is based on Appadurai's concept of five dimensions of global cultural flows (see Chapter 1), and was developed in order to consider simultaneously (1) which scapes are present in individual lives, (2) how individuals use media and communications in and between scapes, and (3) which of these scapes connect or disconnect individuals in different locations.

SCAPES IDENTIFIED

The scapes were identified from two sources: theoretical literature and the materials used for this study. Most of Appadurai's scapes, but not all, were also found in the material collected and some new categories were added during the research process. Table 7.1 shows the issues used in conceptualizing the original scapes.

The materials available supported the existence of all these scapes, although some of the issues were overlapping. Two new scapes which were not in Appadurai's original analysis have been identified: languagescape and timescape. I shall now look at each of the scapes and identify how different categories contribute to each of them. I shall still hold on to my materials, drawing examples from them before leaving them behind.

ETHNOSCAPE

As its name reveals, this has been the main interest for ethnographers. It has also been important to this study, in at least two ways. First, we have seen that individuals' ethnoscapes can change, even if they stay in one place. This has happened in the case of all the families studied. Whilst not moving, the great-grandmother Tyyne lived both in Imperial Russia and in Finland; similarly, the following generations found themselves living both

TABLE 7.1 Scapes in global mediagraphy

Ethnoscape	*Ideoscape*
Home country	Ideology
Location	Resistance
Lifestyle	Identity
Emigration	Interest
	Imagination
Financescape	
Profession	*Timescape*
Class	Age
Family size	Generation
Lifestyle	Calendar
Mediascape	*Languagescape*
Availability of and access to media	Education
Use of media	Knowledge of languages
Technoscape	
Media and communication	

in Finland and in the EU. The first three generations of the Chinese family, whilst not physically moving, lived in different periods in different countries, although staying in place in Dong Xiao Wu. The third family was the only family where one member changed his nationality as a result of physically changing place from Zilupe in Latvia to Kinneret in Palestine/Israel. Even that individual and his descendants, however, although they subsequently remained in the same place, saw their country's borders and designation change from Palestine to Israel.

Secondly, many members of these families have experienced the most violent form of change in ethnoscape: through war. Two generations of the family in Finland, although the country was never in fact occupied, lived for 4 years in fear of occupation. The first two generations of the family in China lived through years of occupation. The Latvian–Israeli family experienced the most devastating consequences of wars: there is not a single generation of this family which has not been affected by conflict. It is also the only family whose members have died because ethnoscapes were on the move.

All three families have also moved place. The first generation of the Finnish family moved from their village to an industrial town. This was the big change for that generation and also caused a shift in lifestyle (from agrarian to industrial). I have thus placed lifestyle under the heading of ethnoscape, as they traditionally come together. The next generation also changed place (from small town to capital city) and accordingly changed lifestyle. The representative of the third generation moved from a national capital to a global capital, and also changed her way of life. All the members of the Finnish family except the youngest have changed their lifestyle by changing places. Only the youngest generation has changed lifestyle while staying in one place. This is where we find the influence of media and communications, their increasing manifestations and availability. The youngest generation of the Finnish family did not need to move, because they have access to the global urban lifestyle in Helsinki. This also connects them with the youngest generation of the other families. They all share in a global youth culture, which connects them across frontiers. Their lifestyle includes films, television, music, videos, the Internet, computer games, fashion and food. This lifestyle is available in Helsinki, Beijing, Tel Aviv or London.

Unlike the Finnish family, the Chinese family stayed in one place for three generations. The youngest generation, however, moved not only from village to capital city, but then from capital to global cities. The youngest member of this family has experienced a more radical change of lifestyle than any of the other individuals studied. Whilst the changes in the Finnish and Chinese families have been in one direction, from small to larger, from the countryside to the city, the Latvian-Israeli family has experienced a 'zigzag' movement, with the second oldest moving back to the countryside and to an agrarian way of life, almost as far as possible from its previous cosmopolitan, urban lifestyle. The Latvian–Israeli family is an example of the reverse flows which take place. This phenomenon can been seen as a form of opposition to globalization and can be found in many parts of the world where, because of their religion or ideology, people 'go back' to a community life in order to protect their way of life and values. The zigzag phenomenon further complicates the linearity of globalization and gives it new time dimensions.

However, the following generation of the Latvian–Israeli family again left the countryside, as its Finnish counterpart had left a generation earlier. Every generation of these three families has experienced at least one big change in lifestyle. Sometimes this has happened within one country, while at other times it has involved emigration to another country. All these families, despite their differences in wealth, class or location, have experienced changes in their lifestyle, which have not only caused changes in their own personal ethnoscapes, but also contributed to globalization.

FINANCESCAPE

All our families have been affected by financescapes, but have themselves also caused changes in these. The Finnish great-grandparents had to leave their farm in Juva in the 1930s as a result of the Great Depression that affected many countries. The youngest generation's unemployment in the 1990s was the result of a national and global recession, which was intensified by the collapse of the Soviet Union (Finland's traditional trade partner) and which particularly affected young, unskilled men. On the other hand, Finland, as a Nordic welfare society, although declining, has been able to provide at least some support for those who were or are unemployed.

The Chinese family's financial circumstances have been difficult because of the circumstances in their country. The Chinese financescape here is closely interwoven with global economic developments, although the Chinese economy was run as a non-capitalist system. Its original goal was to improve the living conditions of the masses, not to encourage people to acquire personal wealth. One can easily see how difficult it is for individuals to make a drastic economic change in their lives if they live under a communist government that imposes restrictions on private ownership. Only when the restrictions were eased in China under the present new economy did it become possible for the youngest generation to leave and study abroad. Restrictions were also imposed on individuals in autocratic societies such as Imperial Russia, where Jewish people did not have the same rights as other citizens. The situation became worse in Latvia under Soviet occupation, when private ownership was abolished, and fatal under Nazi occupation, when 80 per cent of the Jewish population was killed.

However, individuals in these families have made decisions that have contributed to their personal financescapes. The Finnish great-grandparents lost their farm but, like millions of others, began a new urban life, which in the end gave them opportunities they had never had in their original location. The grandmother Eila left her parents' small industrial town in order to have access to the wider world and, again, lived materially better than her parents. Her daughter Terhi left her country not only to achieve personal happiness but also to improve her working conditions and to earn a better salary. Terhi's son Nyrki is critical of his family's work- and education-oriented lifestyle and aspires to a life where work does not take up so much of one's time. In a way, but this time without moving place, he is mentally going back to a kibbutzim or communist-type lifestyle where money is not considered important. However, for Nyrki money, or the lack of it, is important in that this can affect his access to the urban youth lifestyle he also enjoys. The Chinese son Junjie is the first member of his family to break away from his village, although it was his father who broke the peasant family tradition and became a civil servant. This happened at a time when the Chinese Communist Party had announced that it did not want China to remain excluded from globalization. Junjie has possibilities nobody else in his family has ever had.

In all the families there has been a change in class: an upgrade from farming to entrepreneurship, management, journalism and academia. Three members of our three families are now working/studying in the same institution and can be defined as coming from middle-class families. However, all these families are ordinary families, which have not inherited money or status. Education appears as a major way in which the members of these families have improved their financial situation. One can also see that the movement is not always what one might expect. The various family members have different values and live their lives accordingly. This, in turn, connects the financescape with the ideoscape.

MEDIASCAPE

One of the problems in doing research on mediascape is that it easily becomes very technological. Mediascape has many dimensions, however, and technology is only one of these. Defining globalization through connectivity, it is easy to forget that mediascape is not only a question of access, although it is access that makes the rest possible. In my analysis I have not separated media and communications. This separation is one of the weaknesses of Appadurai's scapes: mediascape and technoscape are so close to each other that it is very difficult to separate them. Appadurai, in defining his mediascape, rightly underlines the importance of images as specific to media, but in the present phase of convergence images are also transmitted by instruments of communication such as computers. This decision has resulted, in this analysis, in a very thin technoscape covering only transportation and technological gadgets.

One of the most important findings in this study concerns unequal access to media. This is especially true when we compare countries like Finland (and Israel) with China. In Finland, all our family members have had access to media, whilst in China there is a considerable difference between different family members. There is little difference between individuals' access to media as a result of class. All members of our families had access to media and communications, even if for some of them this was via public gateways such as libraries. The youngest members of the Finnish family do not have their own personal computers, but instead use public libraries, Internet cafés and their friends' computers. There is also no difference between different generations or between genders in terms of media and communication literacy: all three generations use computers and mobile phones.

The Finnish family's situation reflects an average level of resources and wealth in Finland. In China, although an increasing number of people already have access to the latest media and communications, the majority of the population have not. That said, it is important to acknowledge that access to media and communications has rapidly increased and continues to do so. In August 2003, there were 68 million Internet users in China, 8.9 million more than during the first part of the year. China has the second highest number of Internet users in the world, exceeded only by the USA (Mykkänen, 2003). However, in a society like China, class, gender and education play a much bigger role than in countries like Finland. Only 10 per cent of all the Internet users in China are over 40 years of age.

Through access to media and communications, people also gain access to images. Here we see the most convincing proof of homogenization: all our families, despite their location, have been, are and will be increasingly exposed to similar images, many of them still originating from the West. This is a factor that without doubt unites families in Finland, China and Israel. Our families all watch many films and television programmes produced in the United States and the United Kingdom. This does not mean that they only watch programmes and films from these countries, but they all watch them in addition to programmes from their own country or from other countries. The programmes from the USA and the UK are the global content they are most likely to share. Television programmes and films shown on television are the content that also unites different generations: they may not watch the same programmes, but they are able to recognize them. A good example is 'Dallas' in Finland: the mother Terhi watched it when it was originally shown, and her son Nyrki 20 years later, after it became a popular programme among young men in Finland when Finnish television started to show it in the afternoon. Despite his political orientation, the Chinese father Qinghe's favourite programmes are serials. Transnational television culture penetrates borders, nationalities, gender and education. It is everywhere that people have access.

This also applies to news, whether televised, broadcasted or printed. All our families learned about events that shook the world, such as 11 September 2001, mainly through media and communications. Even if they hear about them from other people, they turn to the media to see the images or to learn more. They all share these particular news items about wars, terrorism, famines, catastrophes and crises. The members of the families all now have access to world news, whether through newspapers, radio, television or the Internet. Most of them receive their news through a national medium, although those who live in London use both British and their own national media. Of course, international news is only part of the national media companies' agenda, and most news is national and local. However, the fact that they all have access to the global girdle of news is important as such and connects them to each other. The same global media companies, such as CNN or Reuters, deliver most of the news available to people in different locations.

What applies to television does not necessarily apply to other media and communications. Music is also transnational: we have seen how the youngest generations of our families have been influenced by Anglo-American rock culture, which has also influenced even some of their parents. They are all able to recognize, and even memorize, many of the same songs. Music also divides people: in all three countries national music enjoys great popularity, whether Chinese pop opera, Israeli pop or Finnish rock. The words are Chinese, Hebrew or Finnish, but the music is probably often a mixture of different cultural origins. The different generations also have different tastes in music: the Finnish family's grandmother still prefers German *Schlagers*, her daughter music from her youth, and her son black music. Even the members of the youngest generations in different countries do not necessarily all listen to the same music: there are so many different variations of contemporary music, enabling listeners to form their own distinctive tastes and identities.

The same is true of films, although when films are shown on television they become accessible even to people who would not have bought a ticket to see them at the cinema. Again, we see that there is a shared core of films which almost 'everybody' sees: films like the James Bond series or *The Lord of the Rings*. Many members of our families would be able to discuss these films, although none would probably list them as their very favourite. Films are another item that connects these families.

What is missing from the analysis of many globalization theorists is the consequences of increased access to media and communications. What do people do with the messages they receive? Do these messages merely connect them, or do they constitute a real influence on thinking or consciousness? If they do, this brings us to ideoscapes, and how individuals may have been influenced by the different ideoscapes of their generation.

IDEOSCAPE

Appadurai writes that ideoscapes are often directly political, and frequently have to do with the ideologies of states and the counter-ideologies of movements explicitly oriented to capturing state power or a piece of it. At the most general level there have been ideologies which have touched every one of our families, namely democracy, capitalism, communism, nationalism. All the families have experienced these in one form or another, whether as a state ideology or a counter-ideology. Two generations of the Finnish family lived in the shadow of the communism associated with the Soviet Union and felt as a threat to newly independent Finland. The whole Chinese family, from the great-grandfather to the son, have lived a part of their lives under a communist state. The Latvian–Israeli family have never lived in a communist state (except the great-grandfather under Soviet occupation in 1941), but the family was greatly affected by the struggle between communism and both fascism and capitalism.

Interestingly – and I come back to this when discussing timescape – the very same ideologies have also been counter-ideologies in our same families. In reaction to the anti-communism of her family, the Finnish mother Terhi became active in the leftist youth movement when she was young. Probably nothing could have shocked her family more than her activism. The Latvian grandfather Lasik who emigrated to Palestine opposed his father's values by turning to socialist Zionism, which led him to leave his family and start a new life in a new country. The Chinese father Qinghe became a keen supporter of Chairman Mao and rejected his father's religion.

Capitalism has now reached all the countries that these families have lived or live in: Russia, Finland, Latvia, China and Israel. The Chinese Communist Party still holds power, but has also accepted capitalism as a form of production. Capitalism has not necessarily brought democracy, although the two have sometimes been seen as going hand in hand. Capitalism has also served as a counter-ideology in communist countries, where citizens have sought not only more political freedom as voters but also economic freedom as consumers. Of all ideologies, it is capitalism that has spread more widely than any other. In this sense, homogenization theorists are correct: globalization and capitalism seem to go hand in glove.

Democracy, when defined as universal suffrage, has triumphed in many places. The Finnish great-grandmother Tyyne was 1 year old when the Finns gained the right to vote in 1906, and Finland was still a part of the Russian Empire. Finland was the third country in the world (after New Zealand in 1893 and Australia in 1902) to give women the right to vote. The Jewish great-grandfather Moshe and his wife achieved the right to vote in 1918, when Latvia became independent. That was the first time Jews were given full citizenship rights there. In 1948, with the formation of the state of Israel, women received full suffrage. When the People's Republic of China was founded in 1949, Chinese women gained the right to vote, although they could only vote for one party. Interestingly, after centuries of struggle for universal suffrage, many members of these families do not seem to be interested in using it. Many of them have become disillusioned with politics. This is also one of the scapes of our present time: not only belief, but also disbelief, in ideologies.

Religion, albeit in very different forms, has also been an important factor in the lives of the families. As with political participation, its importance has been in decline. This does not mean that it has no role in the ideoscape, because it continues to hold its position as a source of ideas, even if it is not practised actively. At the same time, it does not have the power it used to have in individual lives, but it has become one of the sources instead of being the only source.

Nationalism is another ideology that has touched all these families. The Finnish great-grandfather Antti spent 4 years at the front. The brother of the Latvian grandfather Lasik was killed in 1948 only 10 days after he arrived at kibbutz Ein-Gev near kibbutz Kinneret, after having narrowly escaped the atrocities in Latvia. The brother of the Israeli family's daughter Shani may be forced to fight for Israeli nationalism any day. In China, the great-grandfather Baosheng hid his family from the occupiers. Nationalism, as many have noted, has probably caused more death than any other ideology.

Nationalism has many faces and has been indigenized as an ideology around the world. Again, we see similarities and differences not only between generations, but between families. The Finnish family presents a kind of Gellnerian European case in which nationhood is constructed through territory, culture and language(s), which are all connected with each other. However, the Finnish great-grandmother Tyyne spent her early childhood in a Grand Duchy of the Russian Empire before becoming, at the age of 11, a citizen of independent Finland. The Israeli national identity was developed from a distance without direct experience of the connection between land and culture. The Chinese family only started to think of themselves in nationalistic terms when they experienced occupation. Most members of the three families have lived in several states, or alliances of states, without moving place. Of the 12 members of our three families, only the Chinese son Junjie and the Israeli daughter Shani have so far been subjects/citizens of just one country. Even in the Finnish case, the three living generations of the family all became citizens of the European Union through an election.

Still, in most cases, their national identity is alive and well, although also contested. It is especially poignant in the Israeli case, where the rights of Palestinian people contradict the legitimacy of the exclusive Israeli national identity that is now based on the relationship between one territory, culture, language and religion, which excludes the Palestinians. But even in the Finnish case, the Finnish mother Terhi has also felt uncomfortable in her homogeneous home country, where Finnishness is often celebrated as a superb way of life, leaving little space for people who do not share its uncontested values. Her mother Eila and her children, in contrast to herself, feel very comfortable with their Finnish identity and are deeply rooted in place. Her children, however, while deeply rooted in their place, are also connected to the wider world through their interest in popular culture.

There is also another level, which has little do with the 'big' ideoscapes and more to do with personal ideoscapes and personal interests. Sometimes the same interests pass from one generation to another; sometimes there is a clear break between two generations; while at other times a child may go back to the generation before his/her parents, ignoring their interests and rediscovering something that was not passed directly to the next generation. In the Chinese family, interest in traditional Chinese opera and calligraphy was passed through two generations, to be interrupted by interest in Western television series, enthusiastically watched by a follower of Chairman Mao. In the Finnish family, an interest in books and music goes from one generation to the next, although personal tastes in these vary. In the Latvian–Israeli family there is an interest in geography, which has been passed from one generation to the next.

These personal ideoscapes – or interestscapes – offer a kind of escape from other scapes, a setting of one's mind on something completely different, an escape from one's locality, one's national space and sometimes from one's family. Very often this is provided by media and communications, as will be explained when I discuss mediascapes. The body is somewhere, but the mind can be anywhere else, such as in the Caribbean Islands on a rainy night in London. As Appadurai (1998: 22) observes, there is a link between the work of the imagination and the emergence of a post-national world. Ideoscapes have traditionally been the most important, but they are complemented and also challenged by individuals' interestscapes. And there is one further scape connected to ideoscapes and interestscapes – the imaginationscapes that individuals use to 'travel' in time and space without moving. Media and communications often provide the ingredients for imaginationscapes.

TECHNOSCAPE

Two of Appadurai's scapes, technoscapes and mediascapes, are understood quite narrowly, mainly in terms of access or images. They are also partly overlapping, since both media and communications are separated into two scapes, although in practice these often go together. As I will show later, this division undermines the importance of media and communications, which are present in every scape and which often serve to bind together different scapes. However, it is important not to altogether lose mediascapes and technoscapes as such, as often happens when we refer to media and communications as mediators. Technoscape includes here both technology that facilitates transportation, and technology that facilitates mediation.

In both contexts, most members of our three families have been much affected by their respective countries' infrastructure. Nation-states have in the past played a determining role in providing and preventing their citizens access to media. To a certain extent this is still the case, as can be very clearly seen in countries such as Finland. As the leading information society in the world, Finland can provide a level of access to its citizens which those in other countries do not have. This has happened as a direct result of government policy aimed at increasing people's access to communications. When schools and libraries provide free access to the Internet and people are computer literate, individual wealth is still a factor, but lack of wealth does not completely exclude individuals from access to communications.

There is also an effect on traditional gender roles. Whilst, according to recent statistics, there are only two countries in the world with more female than male home Internet users (the US with 51.4 per cent and Canada with 51.9 per cent), Finland is among those countries where female users account for between 45 and 50 per cent of all home Internet users (New Zealand has 49.6, Finland 47.0, Australia 46.9, South Korea 45.9, Argentina 45.4, Ireland 45.2, Singapore 45.0 and Taiwan 45.0 per cent).[1]

The promotion of a concept of communication for everybody, as envisaged in Sreberny's (1996) first stage of international communication (see Chapter 4), also creates minds, which are open to the latest technology, as happened when mobile phones were first introduced in Finland. As a result, there are now more mobile phones than people in Finland. Possessing a personal mobile phone is probably as common among 15- to 74-year-old Finns today as having a wristwatch. In the last couple of years mobile phones have also rapidly become common in the under-15 age group, as well as among pensioners. For some time to come, the mobile phone is likely to be seen as the piece of equipment with the fastest spread of almost universal adoption in history.[2]

In the Chinese case, government policy on media and communications has been the opposite to that of Finland, but the situation is rapidly changing. The Communist government sought to control people's access to communication, and managed to do this for 50 years. However, with the rapid development of electronic and digital communication, such control became more and more difficult. Now the Chinese government acknowledges the importance of computer literacy and access in its drive to improve China's global market position. It still imposes control on communications and media, but simply cannot do this in the same way as in the past. According to official figures released by the Ministry of Information Industries, the number of mobile phone subscribers had reached 200.3 million by the end of November 2002. The Ministry also announced that the number of Internet users rose by 2.4 million in November, to nearly 48.3 million.[3]

In Israel in 2002 there were almost 6.3 million mobile phone subscribers representing a penetration rate of 94.7 per cent. Approximately 1200 million text messages were sent (Lopez, 2002). Text messaging has proved, as in Finland, remarkably successful among young people.

TIMESCAPE

What became apparent during the process of this study, but was absent from Appadurai's original scapes, is the significance of time. Timescape encompasses several issues, including time zones, calendars, age, generation, memory and media time.

Zone Time

The most obvious, although surprisingly often ignored, factor is that people live in different time zones. This affects their connectivity, as everybody who has tried to work out the best time to call Los Angeles from London knows. The time shared by people who live in different locations depends on the time zones they live in. Time zones were of course artificially created, as shown in Chapter 3, in order to facilitate communication between people, but are also based on the hours of light and darkness, sleeping and waking. As a result, the time people share is not 24 hours but considerably less, depending on their time zone.

Calendar Time

The other factor that affects people's connectivity is the difference between calendars. Different holidays are observed in different parts of the world. For example, an Israeli student studying in London may observe her Saturday as a holiday, according to the Jewish calendar, but Sunday is observed as a holiday in the UK. The times she can reach people during business hours are limited by holidays, even those which she does not observe. The same is true of different annual holidays, such as Christmas and New Year's Eve.

Generation Time

Another issue that has come up during the research process is people's age and generation as separating and unifying factors in their experiences. This again raises the question of shared time, but in this case time shared by different generations. Two generations may coexist for about 50 years, but three generations probably share only about 30 years. This is the time when generations can interact. Their interaction is, however, limited by individuals' life stages: whether they are very young or very elderly has a considerable effect on their interaction. There is also a period of each individual's life, their childhood, to which the next generation has no access. As a result, there are always memories and experiences one cannot share even with the members of one's own family.

Once we acknowledge this difference, it is much easier to understand the differences in ideoscapes within each of these families. Accordingly, we can see that people in different localities can share experiences and memories simply because they belong to the same generation. For example, two or three generations of our three families have all experienced war, whilst only one member of the fourth generation has any experience of it. This experience is a very formative one, and difficult to share with somebody whose life has not been under such direct threat. On the other hand, the fourth generation's experience of extensive mediated globalization is very difficult to share with previous generations, who are often completely ignorant of the music, films and television programmes shared by the youngest generation, wherever they are located.

There is also forgotten time when an individual or a generation does not want to remember. There are voids when certain memories have not been transferred to the next generation because they have been suppressed. As Zerubavel (2003: 89) notes, there are *rites of separation* that are specifically designed to dramatize the symbolic transformations of identity involved in establishing new beginnings, essentially implying that it is possible to 'turn over a new leaf' or somehow be 'reborn'. This is most obvious in the Latvian–Israeli family, when even a whole language was 'forgotten', but is also visible in the 'new' beginnings of independent Finland or communist China.

Personal Time

One's personal time is affected by work, but also by one's inner time. Most people, especially those who are active in work life and live in global cities, suffer from lack of time, the feeling that they are constantly running against time. Of course, parents of small children or students also lack time, whatever their location. A personal sense of time is often formed by one's previous experience. The members of the three families often talk about how busy life in London is compared with their home locations, even if these are in the capital cities of their home countries. They miss their countries or their own language and enjoy the experience of going back home and slowing down. They can clearly see the difference between their sense of time and that of other members of their families. They also want to have time of their own, when they cannot be reached by communications. One way to get time of their own is to watch television or listen to the radio and not 'hear' what is going on around them.

Media Time

It is the media that create the experience of global shared time, especially by informing people around the world about 'events' that they can share. It is the media that penetrate holy days and nights because they have the ability to do so. Whatever the time, one can always tune in to electronic media if one has access to them. Communications give people a chance to contact other people in distant locations whatever the time.

Languagescape

Yet another factor which does not emerge as an independent scape in Appadurai's analysis is the role of language as a separating or uniting factor. As long as people do not share a language, it is very difficult for them to interact. If we look at the three families, the first members who could potentially communicate across frontiers would have been the Latvian great-grandfather Moshe and the Finnish grandmother Eila since they both spoke German. However, there is a considerable age difference and Eila, in her early teens, would probably not have had sufficient language skills to have a proper conversation in German with Moshe. His grandson Nechemya and the Finnish grandmother Eila would have been able to speak to each other, although her English was at the time not as good as her German. Neither of them would have been able to speak to any members of the Chinese family if they had met them. In the Chinese family, the son's generation is the first to reach out and speak to three generations of the other families.

This has been made possible by the spread around the world of English as a second language. Although not the most widespread language, it has increasingly become the language of politics, economics and culture. As shown in Chapter 6, however, people speak English in many different ways and with many different accents. English is a homogenizing factor, but its widespread use in different locations has also heterogenized the language. One could scarcely expect people in different locations all to speak the Queen's English. English is spoken in distinctively different ways around the world, as it is in our three families.

Those members of the three families who live in London and speak English as their primary language on a daily basis have achieved a degree of fluency that makes them bilingual. However, when asked, all of them would point out the difficulties in expressing themselves compared with English native speakers. The Finnish mother Terhi, who teaches in English, finds that she will never speak as freely and express herself as well as her colleagues who are native speakers. She still has to get her her scholarly writings in English corrected before submitting them. Shani, Junjie and Terhi all need to concentrate more when they speak English, compared with their native languages. When they get tired or upset, their English becomes weaker or occasionally disappears. English is definitely a language they have learned and they feel that they can never use it to express their innermost, most intimate thoughts. When they feel like that, they have a tendency to return from cosmopolitanism to a zone of safety, as described in Chapter 6.

When they agonize about their English, they tend to forget that they have achieved something most English speakers have not: they speak more than one language. There is no way any of them, and especially the members of the Finnish family (there are only 5 million Finnish speakers), can go to a foreign country and be understood in their own language. In contrast, most English speakers can feel quite confident that somebody will speak their language almost anywhere they go. In that respect, all our family members have qualifications that have made them employable outside their home countries.

In this way, as in other scapes, language becomes a factor which sometimes separates and sometimes unites individuals within mediated globalization. It is an important asset, but it is not the only one. The members of the three families watch the same imported TV programmes in their home countries, with subtitles or voiceover. This is one of the ways in which cultural products are indigenized. Even if they are not able to share the language, they are able to share some images and symbols across frontiers. However, many of these images and symbols are predominantly imported only from a couple of countries, such as the USA and the UK.

WHAT HAS BEEN ACHIEVED?

This book started with the aim of showing the role of media and communications in globalization. In order to understand this role, it was necessary to develop a new methodology which would be sensitive not only to issues of multi-sitedness (globalization taking place in different locations), but also to issues of multiple timeframe (globalization taking place at different speeds). In order to carry out research on this mediated phenomenon and its multiple consequences, a new approach, global mediagraphy, was developed in an effort to capture some of the key elements of globalization in the lives of individuals in multiple locations. The components of individual mediagraphies make it possible to compare the lives of individuals, not only within one generation, but also across different generations in different places. The completed family mediagraphies are shown in Tables 7.2–7.4

Taking a family, rather than a single individual, as the starting point also builds a bridge between macro- and micro-levels, since families are basic units of society and an interface between the public and the private. At the same time, every family is unique, both different from and similar to every other family, since each is based on certain relationships (parent–child, parent–parent, child–parent) and on the role of families in society. Many of the ideological struggles are fought within families, where traditions are both broken and maintained.

There are also significant differences between families. In two of our three case studies (Israeli, Chinese) we followed the paternal line, while in the Finnish family we followed the maternal line until the fourth generation. Gender obviously plays a big role in these families. It is fair to say that the picture would have been different if we had followed the maternal line in all three cases. I have 'tested' mediagraphies with individual students from different countries since starting this project, and I have noticed that when students have not been able to track their grandparents, they have included both their parents instead. The picture, and the comparison, become more complicated, but also add a new dimension and introduce the complexity of the 'globalization of love'. As shown in Chapter 6, everyday cosmopolitanism is often invisible and is executed in families, often by women.

One could also be critical of the middle-class bias in our three families. Because of the university connection between three family members, the materials are somewhat 'biased'. That said, in two of the families, the Chinese and the Finnish, access to education and to the middle class has been relatively recent and/or temporary.

One could also be critical of the limitation of the materials. The research is based on three families that could be conventionally labelled as 'Finnish', 'Latvian–Israeli' and 'Chinese'. This is, however, only one way of identifying them. In the Israeli case, for instance, the Israeli nationality can only be used to identify the whole lives of two family members. Even in the case of more 'stable' families, such as the Chinese and the Finnish, one nationality is not enough to describe them. In the Chinese case, there is a divided Chinese identity (mainland China versus Taiwan), and an identity of the youngest generation on the move. In the Finnish family, there is an extended family with Finnish, British and Sri Lankan origins and identities. Even those members of all three families who have remained in one place have experienced many changes in the countries of their birth. In short, the history of nation-states is very brief and unstable. Even further, one can be a resident, citizen or subject of a certain country, for example China, but this does not make one Chinese. Or one can be Chinese, but live somewhere else. One nationality is enough to identify a person, but hyphenated nationalities have become much more common. Nationality is like gender: it is used as the most general label but does not reveal what is beyond that.

TOWARDS THEORIZATION OF MEDIAGRAPHIES

The materials collected in mediagraphies both complement and contradict theories of globalization and the role of media and communications within these. However, it is now time to leave 'the micro' aside and to start thinking about how mediagraphies contribute to our understanding of globalization theories.

First, a significant contribution is that when we understand that people's nationality is only one of their identities, and not necessarily the most significant one in their daily life, we see that the juxtaposition between the 'international' and the 'national' is coming to an end as the single point of departure for any research. Of course, this is what globalization theorists have been saying for more than a decade now, but only by looking at the lives of individuals in different locations can we fully understand the similarities between their lives. There are no winners in nationalism, but all suffer from it even if not simultaneously. At one time a nation is an invader, at another it is being invaded. Individuals are invited to form attachments to nation-states, but these nation-states are constantly changing their boundaries and thus redefining themselves. They need to invite people to share their particular nationalism and to use media and communications to mediate between them and individuals.

Earlier, before the development of electronics, media and communications could be restricted within one country, although there were always leaks. These leaks started working against nationalism, which relied on the holy trinity of territory, people and culture. Nationalism has never been able to execute fully its key idea of the union between the three, but instead has always violated the rights of the people who are in the minority in any given country. However, in trying to invite people to share the idea of nationhood, it uses homogeneity as an incentive.

It is important to understand that media and communications have both contributed to nation-building and globalization and continue to do so. But because national spaces have become much more open, it is difficult to keep any space purely national. When the scapes are on the move, media and communication often play a decisive role. Their crucial role is visible not only within, but also across, different scapes. Media and communication become the factors that connect one scape to another. They contribute significantly to the flows Appadurai refers to. They are also the factors connecting individuals in their respective locations to one another, even when they remain physically far apart. This connection, whether between individuals or between scapes, is never simply a connection but is always mediated and thus loaded with meanings. This is why media and communications never just connect: they are never just transmitters in a vacuum, but operate in spaces where the air is thick with meanings.

As Appadurai has suggested, as a result of the scapes being on the move there are junctures and disjunctures. This makes perfect sense, but remains a very general statement. If we want to understand the specific historical circumstances in which they occur, we need to look at individuals and their lives. Here we find some of the junctures and disjunctures in their lives, as experienced from below. However, this has a connection with the macro-level. We can understand how the macro and the micro come together and cause the major changes in both of them.

What we need to look for are those instances where not only do junctures or disjunctures occur, but there is an opportunity for individuals to make a change, to become an agent. Doing research on individuals in different locations, across borders, we can identify those where an unexpected juncture or disjuncture takes place that will become a major flow later. Often there is a connection, an almost invisible rhizome that then contributes to a major change in the movement between and within the scapes. We can see things that are emerging only when we look at the lives of individuals in multiple locations.

One of the problems with Appadurai's scapes is that they provide a rather flat landscape. There is no time dimension and thus no past. The analysis captures how scapes work here and now. However, changes in scapes occur at different times around the world. It is thus crucially important to do historical research to understand how timescapes occur. Time, although increasingly overcome by media and communications, still plays a significant role, sometimes causing delays in both junctures and disjunctures.

Differences in the timing of globalization become clear when we consider individual mediagraphies. In Chapter 2, I referred to Robertson's division of globalization theories into five different stages and added a new one: the stage of antagonism. It is clear that countries such as China were excluded from Robertson's 'take-off stage', which he defined as starting in the 1870s and lasting until the 1920s. China clearly did not share many of the features Robertson describes as characteristic of the period. It was, however, touched by world events such as World War I. In fact, the factor that has touched most individuals in our three families has been war, or the threat of war. For many people, globalization becomes a present reality when their countries are either invaded or face the threat of invasion.

De-territorialization contests not only the traditional thinking of land and culture tied together, but also the idea of geographical territories matching people's citizenships, nationalities and identities. Increasingly, because of media and communications, people are able to live in different spaces that may match with their locations, but are also able to reach out. The fact that people have been able to reach out of their locations through media and communications to share a national space indicates that they could go even further to share a global space.

Sharing a global space can never be similar to the *ideal* of a neighbourhood. The same concerns the ideal of nationhood, if it is defined as comradeship among equals. Relationships are seldom equal, even in the neighbourhood. Landowners and peasants, factory owners and workers, may live in the same neighbourhood, but their relationships are far from equal. The same concerns relationship across a nation or across the globe. The ideal of *united nations* is not realistic, but the *ideal* of individuals united beyond nation-states is emerging.

However, at this moment all our families are involved in the current stage of globalization – that of antagonism. I am writing this concluding chapter in 2003 on the fourth day of the invasion of Iraq by the coalition army. Each member of our families reacts to this event, consumers as they all are of the media, which have given us 'artificial eyes but no arms'. Our family members watch the images of war transmitted by global television companies to their respective locations, and react to these in accordance with their own political stance. Many members of our three families have demonstrated against the war in their own locations and seen pictures of other anti-war demonstrations around the world. Globalization from above and below go as hand in hand, but clearly there is no question about who has more power in this situation.

This again brings into the picture the question of whether the main consequence of globalization is homogenization or heterogenization. It is not only the military power of the USA, and to a lesser degree of the UK, which is currently so visible, but also their media power. The resources and technology at the disposal of the global media companies to cover the war is overwhelming in comparison with any other media company. The war is being reported in such detail that it gives viewers the illusion that they can follow the coalition troops step by step. The helplessness felt by many of our family members as they watch these pictures is reinforced by the intensity of the coverage. At the same time, as they watch they do not want to see, because the identification with the suffering of those being hurt or killed is almost too much to bear. The current phase of antagonism is intensified by modern media, which give us this sense of the 'global village'. Without the media we would not know about the progress of the war almost minute by minute. But what if we do not like what we see? The global village is so huge that we can only see our neighbours; we cannot touch them. This, in turn, raises the question of the rights and responsibilities of people who do not fit the role of citizens of one country. In what context should we hear their words? Or see their actions? For what – or to whom – are they responsible? These are the questions we have only started to theorize, because we have only recently become aware of them.

It would be easy, under these circumstances, to end this book quite pessimistically. However, the last 100 years in the lives of our three families have shown incredible events, hard circumstances, violence and grief, but also endurance, survival, resistance and joy. None of these families are similar to each other, but increasingly they share a consciousness of the world that goes beyond traditional frontiers. Doing exercises such as mediagraphies helps us to reflect not only on our own lives, but also on the lives of other people across space and time.

TABLE 7.2 Family 1: completed mediagraphy

	Great-grandmother Tyyne, 1905–87	Grandmother Eila, 1927–	Mother Terhi, 1953–	Son Nyrki, 1976–
Profession	Peasant, industrial worker, shopkeeper	Journalist	Academic	Printer
Home country	Imperial Russia, Finland	Finland, EU citizenship from 1995	Finland, UK, EU citizenship from 1995	Finland, EU citizenship from 1995
Place	Rural village in Juva, industrial town of Kotka	Juva, Kotka, small towns, capital Helsinki, Kotka	Small town of Lappeenranta, Helsinki, global city of London	Helsinki
Time	Gregorian and Julian calendar	Gregorian calendar	Gregorian calendar	Gregorian calendar
Changes in lifestyle	From rural to urban	From rural to urban	From capital to cosmopolitan	Capital
Education	4 years + 1 year (professional course in agricultural husbandry)	11 years + 2 years (professional course in journalism, unfinished)	12 years + 18 years Journalist	11 years so far
Changes in class	From peasantry to petty bourgeoisie	From petty bourgeoisie to middle class	From middle class to professional middle class	From middle class to skilled working class
Family	Eleven siblings (two died as infants) Father died when Tyyne was 5 Stepfather	Two sisters (one died as an infant)	No siblings Two stepmothers One stepfather	One brother plus two sisters from father's second marriage Two brothers from mother's second marriage One stepmother and one stepfather
Travel	Nordic countries, Europe, USA	Nordic countries, Europe, N. America, S. America, Australia, Africa	Nordic countries, Europe, N. America, Asia, Australia, Africa	Nordic countries, Europe, N. America, Asia, Australia, Africa
First overseas journey	At age 63 to Norway	At age 20 to Sweden	At age 10 to Sweden	At age 3 to Sweden

TABLE 7.2 *Cont.*

	Great-grandmother Tyyne, 1905–87	Grandmother Eila, 1927–	Mother Terhi, 1953–	Son Nyrki, 1976–
Languages spoken	Finnish	Finnish, Swedish, German, English	Finnish, English, Swedish, Russian	Finnish, English
Media and communication	Books from 1920, newspapers from birth, radio from 1935, magazines from 1938, film from 1936, phone from 1939, television from 1964	Books, newspapers from birth, magazines, radio from early childhood, phone from 1951, television from 1963, video from 1987, computer from 1980 (work), mobile phone from 1994, Internet from 1998	Books, newspapers, magazines, radio, phone from birth, television from 1963, record player from 1967, video from 1987, computer from 1990, Internet from 1990, mobile phone from 1996	Books, newspapers, magazines, radio, television from birth, video, computer from early childhood, mobile phone from 1996
Interests	Knitting, reading, gardening, religion, radio and television	Reading, radio, television, gardening, classical music, theatre, golf	Reading, exercise, music (pop and classical), movies, gardening	Black music (soul, funk), television, videos, reading, football
Ideology	Lutheran, agrarian, voted regularly	Social democrat, secular non-partisan, votes regularly	Disillusioned leftist, no longer interested in party politics, does not vote, secular but member of the Finnish Lutheran Church	Green, not interested in party politics but votes occasionally, secular
Resistance to	Communism, Soviet Union, idleness and drunkenness	Communism, Soviet Union, women's unequal pay, idleness and drunkenness	War in Vietnam 1961–75, Chilean coup 1973, Cold War, patriarchy, drunkenness, idleness	Compulsory national military service Protestant work ethic
Identity	Local, national	Local, national and cosmopolitan	Local and cosmopolitan	Local, national, cosmopolitan

TABLE 7.3 Family 2: completed mediagraphy

	Great-grandfather Baosheng, 1888–1971	Grandfather Zhansheng, 1923–2000	Father Qinghe, 1944–	Son Junjie, 1974–
Profession	Peasant	Peasant	Peasant, civil servant	Journalist
Home country	China under Qing Dynasty until 1912, Republic of China 1912–49, Japanese occupation 1937–45, People's Republic of China 1949–	Republic of China 1912–49, Japanese occupation 1937–45, People's Republic of China 1949–	Republic of China 1912–49, Japanese occupation 1937–45, People's Republic of China 1949–	People's Republic of China
Place	Dong Xiao Wu village	Dong Xiao Wu village	Dong Xiao Wu village and Ci County	Dong Xiao Wu village, Ci County, Beijing, London, Los Angeles
Time	First only Chinese, later Gregorian and Chinese calendars	Gregorian and Chinese calendars	Gregorian and Chinese calendars	Gregorian and Chinese calendars
Changes in lifestyle	From feudalism to socialism	More diversified rural life than previous generation	From rural to urban	From rural to capital and to cosmopolitan
Education	Primary school	3 years primary school and junior school	8 years primary and junior middle school	13 + 4 (undergraduate) + 2 (postgraduate)
Changes in class	None (peasantry)	None (peasantry)	From peasantry to middle class (but collective)	None (middle class)
Family	Four siblings	Four siblings	Seven siblings	Three siblings
Travel	Some places in China	Many places in China	Many places in China	China, UK, USA
First overseas journey	Never	Never	Never	At the age of 27 to UK, then US
Languages spoken	Chinese dialect	Chinese dialect	Chinese dialect	Chinese dialect, Mandarin, English

TABLE 7.3 *Cont.*

	Great-grandfather Baosheng, 1888–1971	Grandfather Zhansheng, 1923–2000	Father Qinghe, 1944–	Son Junjie, 1974–
Media and communication	Government loudspeaker installed at home in people's commune in the 1960s, books from 1900s, film from 1950s, radio from 1960s	Books from 1930s, newspaper seldom, radio from 1960s often, magazines seldom, film from 1950s, telephone from 1990s, television from 1980s computer never	Books from 1940s, newspapers 1950s, radio 1960s, magazines 1950s, film 1950s, phone 1980s, television 1970s, computer and Internet sometimes	Books 1970s, newspapers 1980s, radio 1980s, magazines 1980s, film 1980s, television 1980s (first private TV set in 1985), computer and Internet 1990s
Interests	Chinese traditional opera, books, Chinese calligraphy	Chinese traditional opera, Chinese traditional fiction books, radio, television series	Television series, television news	Chinese calligraphy, Western classical music, playing basketball
Ideology	Traditional Confucianism	Taoism and Confucianism	Socialism and a fan of Chairman Mao, atheist	Liberal cosmopolitan with a strong Chinese national identity, disappointed with any ideology Previously an atheist like his father but now his attitude to religion has been gradually changed to be more tolerant to different religions His mother also believes in Taoism
Resistance to:		Foreign television programmes, any advertisement on the television	Capitalism	Inequality, cynical about all current social systems
Identity	Chinese, peasant, local	Chinese, peasant, local	Chinese, local to national	Chinese, local to national to cosmopolitan

TABLE 7.4 Family 3: completed mediagraphy

	Great-grandfather Moshe, 1881–1941	Grandfather Lasik, 1912–97	Father Nechemya, 1941–	Daughter Shani, 1972–
Profession	Draper	Peasant	Manager	Academic
Home country	Latvia	Latvia, Palestine, Israel	Palestine, Israel	Israel
Place	Small town Zilupe (20,000 people)	Zilupe in Latvia, kibbutz (rural) in Kinneret	Kibbutz, cities around the world, back to towns in Israel	Kibbutz, cities abroad, back to Israel, then to London
Time	Hebrew and Julian calendars	First Julian and then Hebrew calendars	Hebrew and Gregorian calendars when abroad	Gregorian and Hebrew calendars
Changes in lifestyle	No changes	From urban diasporic lifestyle to collective lifestyle of kibbutz (rural)	From collective lifestyle (rural) to private, urban lifestyle	From collective lifestyle (rural) to urban lifestyle, from local to international/global
Education	Jewish education in the 'heder'	12 years high school	12 years high school	12 years high school + 7.5 years higher education
Changes in class	None (middle class all his life)	From peasantry to middle class (collective)	None (middle class)	None (middle class)
Family	Three sisters	Two brothers, one sister	Three brothers	Two brothers, one sister
Travel	None	Russia, Finland, Estonia, Lithuania (at age 20), Germany, Belgium, France (at age 60)	Kenya, Cyprus (20), South Africa (25), USA, Czechoslovakia, Ethiopia (25–34), Turkey (34), Western Europe (36)	Turkey (5), Europe (7–22), USA (23), Latin America (23)
First overseas journey	None	As a teenager to the Baltic countries	At age 20, leisure trip to Cyprus	At age 5, to Turkey (part of father's work commission)
Languages spoken	Russian, Yiddish, Latvian, basic Hebrew (only for prayer purposes)	Latvian, Yiddish, Russian, Hebrew	Hebrew, English, basic French	Hebrew, English

TABLE 7.4 *Cont.*

	Great-grandfather Moshe, 1881–1941	Grandfather Lasik, 1912–97	Father Nechemya, 1941–	Daughter Shani, 1972–
Media and communication	Books (Russian and Yiddish), religious books, daily newspaper in Yiddish, gramophone, telephone (only for business matters, located in the shop)	Books, newspapers, radio, cinema, television (since age 55), public phone (since age 42), domestic phone (since age 63)	Books, newspapers, radio, cinema, public phone (since age 18), VCR (since age 29), computer and Internet (since age 54) mobile phone (since age 59)	Books, newspapers, radio, cinema, television, VCR (since age 10), computer (since age 20), Internet (since age 23), mobile phone (since age 25)
Interests		Geography, history	Flying, geography	Theatre, poetry
Ideology	Jewish non-Zionist, strong identification with the local Jewish community in which he lived all his life	Local socialist, patriotic	Liberal	Cosmopolitan with a sense of Israeli national identity
Resistance to	Did not approve his son's decision to leave Latvia and join the 'Aliyah' in Israel (driven by Zionist ideology)	Capitalism/ hedonism, opposed to fundamental orthodox religious Jewish	Anti-right-wing, anti-militarism opposed to fundamental orthodox religious Jewish	Anti-right-wing, anti-colonialist (particularly in the Israeli context), opposed to fundamental orthodox religious Jewish

NOTE

1 http://www.etcnewmedia.com/review/default.asp?SectionID=100, 15 October 2002.
2 http://www.stat.fi/tk/yr/tietoyhteiskunta/matkapuhelin.htm/, 10 August 2003.
3 http://www.nua.ie/surveys/index.cgi?f=VS&artid=905358668&res=true, 24 March 2003.

ACKNOWLEDGEMENTS

Mitt hysteriska land, mitt olyckligt älskade väsensfrämmande egna land![1]
—minun hysteerinen maani, onnettomasti rakastamani, minulle vieras oma maani![2]
(My hysterical country, my unhappily beloved own but foreign country.)

Marianne Alopaeus

It takes a village to write a book, in this case a global village. This book owes much to one institution and to several individuals in different locations. The institution is the London School of Economics and Political Science in London. Without the School's commitment under the leadership of Professor Tony Giddens to issues of globalization, I would never have been able to develop my own ideas about the role of media and communication. Specifically, the book owes much to the MSc Programme in Global Media and Communications which I have directed since its inception in 2000, and to one of its two core courses Media and Globalization, which I have been teaching since then.

Of all the individuals needed to collect materials I am most grateful to my former students, Shani Orgad and Junjie Song. They have generously given their time and answered my questions. I am also deeply indebted to their family members who have assisted the project in various ways. Shani and Junjie have both commented on different drafts of the manuscript and given their invaluable insights. However, the interpretations are mine, and they or any other participants in this project are not in any way responsible for these.

Shani – one of the first 12 students to take my course when it was run as a pilot – has been a seminar teacher on the course every year since, and now as a member of the academic staff of the newly founded Department of Media and Communications, has become a full-time colleague. Without her contribution and that of other teaching assistants (Dr Cornel Sandvoss, Philippe Ross, Dr Henrik Örnebring, Gavin Adams and Patrick McCurdy) it would have been impossible to run courses where over 100 students have completed their mediagraphies. Our students from all over the world, with their sharp criticism, have helped me to improve my ideas. It has been a pleasure to work with all of you.

My very special thanks go to Jean Morris for editing my language with professionalism and wit and for being a good colleague and friend. Julia Hall, Jamilah Ahmed, Fabienne Pedroletti of Sage, the copyeditor Brian Goodale and Professor James Lull have been very helpful and improved my book with their thoughtful criticism. I am also grateful to my colleagues in the Department of Media and Communications, especially Professor Roger Silverstone and Dr Nick Couldry, for their comments. Many people, including Tamar Ashuri, Kai Bücher, Armida de la Garza, Terttu Kaivola, Timo Laukkanen, Dr Hillel Nossek, Dr Panu Pulma, Professor Jean Seaton and Professor Daya Thussu, have also helped with information and comments.

As every migrant knows, making a new life in a new country is not always easy. Richard, my husband, has given me his support in ways, which I have not always even noticed. He has made me a member of a 'British' family where both my sisters-in-law share my 'otherness' and which has welcomed the latest newcomer with warmth and acceptance. Thank you, the Collins family! Dr Paula Saukko of Exeter University has given me not only her critical comments but also her support as a friend while we both work as academic 'Gastarbeiterinnen' in the UK. Carol Whitwill was among the first friends in a new country and helped more than she knows.

Ulla Ekebom, my friend I have known since I was seven, is present on many pages of this book, as are many of my other close and often missed friends, especially those who used to live or still live in Kruunuhaka. The loss of Mariankatu 15a A 19 is never forgotten! Ulla and her husband, Jelle, however, generously open their home whenever I visit Helsinki.

I would like to thank my sons, Nyrki and Sampo, for everything including their tolerance of losing their mother to foreign strands, but above all for becoming such fine young men. Kiitos, rakkaimmat! I had a close relationship with my grandmother, Tyyne, who used to tell me stories about the time when she was young. My mother, Eila, and my aunt, Sisko, have followed the same family tradition. I want to thank them for their contribution to this book, but above all I am simply grateful for their love. My mother not only raised me as a single parent, but also gave me an appetite for exploring the world beyond boundaries. As a professional writer herself, she has always been a good and critical commentator. For more reasons than I can mention here: this one is for you, Äiti.

NOTES

1 Alopaeus, M. (1965–1976) *Mörkrets kärna*. Stockholm: Trevi, p. 258.
2 Alopaeus, M. (1965–1971) *Pimeyden ydin*. (Translated by Elvi Sinervo) Jyväskylä: Gummerus., p. 332.

REFERENCES

Albrow, M. (1990) *Globalization, Knowledge and Society: Readings from International Sociology.* London: Sage.

Anderson, B. (1983) *Imagined Communities.* London: Verso.

Appadurai, A. (1990) 'Disjuncture and difference in the global cultural economy', *Public Culture,* 2 (3): 1–23.

Appadurai, A. (1998) *Modernity at Large: Cultural Dimensions of Globalization.* Minneapolis: University of Minnesota Press.

Asante, M.K. and Gudykunst, W.B. (eds) (1989) *Handbook of International and Intercultural Communication.* Newbury Park, CA: Sage.

Augé, M. (1995) *Non-Places: Introduction to an Anthropology of Supermodernity.* London: Verso.

Barker, C. (1997) *Global Television: An Introduction.* Oxford: Blackwell.

Bauman, Z. (2001) 'Quality and inequality', *The Guardian,* 29 December.

Beck, U. (2000a) *What is Globalization?* Cambridge: Polity.

Beck, U. (2000b) *The Brave New World of Work.* Malden, MA: Polity.

Beck, U. (2002) 'The cosmopolitan society and its enemies', *Theory, Culture & Society,* 19 (1–2): 17–44.

Beck–Gernsheim, E. (2002) *Reinventing the Family: In Search of New Lifestyles.* Cambridge: Polity.

Beltrán, P. (1976) 'Alien premises: objects and methods in Latin American communications research', *Communications Research,* 3 (2): 107–34.

Beynon, J. and Dunkerley, D. (eds) *Globalization: The Reader.* London: Athlone.

Billig, M. (1995) *Banal Nationalism.* London: Sage.

Boyd-Barrett, O. (1977) 'Media Imperialism: towards an international framework for the analysis of media systems', pp. 116–35 in J. Curran, M. Gurevitch and J. Woollacot (eds) *Mass Communication and Society.* London: Arnold.

Boyd-Barrett, O. (1982) 'Cultural dependency and the mass media', pp. 174–95 in M. Gurevitch et al. (eds) *Culture, Society and the Media.* London: Methuen.

Boyd-Barrett, O. (1998) 'Media imperialism reformulated', pp. 157–76 in D.K. Thussu (ed.) *Electronic Empires: Global Media and Local Resistance.* London: Arnold.

Boyd-Barrett, O. and Rantanen, T. (eds) (1998) *The Globalization of News.* London: Sage.

Burawoy, M. (2000) *Global Ethnography: Forces, Connections, and Imaginations in a Postmodern World.* Berkeley, CA: University of California Press.

Burstein, D. and de Keijzer, A. (1999) *Big Dragon. The Future of China: What It Means for Business, the Economy, and the Global Order.* New York: Touchstone.

Carey, J.W. (1989) *Communication as Culture: Essays on Media and Society.* Boston: Unwin Hyman.

Castells, M. (1993) 'European cities, the information society and the public economy', pp. 319–22 in A. Gray and J. McGuigan (eds) *Studying Culture: An Introductory Reader.* London: Arnold.

Castells, M. (1996) *The Rise of the Network Society.* Oxford: Blackwell.

Castells, M. and Himanen, P. (2001) *Suomen Tietoyhteiskuntamalli.* Helsinki: Werner Söderström Osakeyhtiö.

Cathcart, R. and Gumpert, G. (1986) 'Mediated interpersonal communication: toward a new typology', pp. 26–40 in R. Cathcart and G. Gumpert (eds) *Inter/Media: Interpersonal Communication in a Media World*. New York: Oxford University Press.

Chadha, K. and Kavoori, A. (2000) 'Media imperialism revisited: some findings from the Asian case', in *Media, Culture & Society*, 22 (4) 415–32.

Chang, W.H. (1989) *Mass Media in China: The History and the Future*. Ames, IA: Iowa State Press.

Crang, M. (1998) *Cultural Geography*. London: Routledge.

De Certeau, M. (1984) *The Practice of Everyday Life*. Berkeley, CA: University of California Press.

Deibert, R.J. (1997) *Parchment, Printing, and Hypermedia: Communication in World Order Transformation*. New York: Columbia University Press.

Deleuze, G. and Guattari, F. (1976) *Rhizome: Introduction*. Paris: Éditions de Minuit.

Ellis, C. and Bochner, A. (2000) 'Autoethnography, personal narrative, reflexivity: researcher as subject', pp. 733–68 in N.K. Denzin and Y. Lincoln (eds) *Handbook of Qualitative Research*, 2nd edn. Thousand Oaks, CA: Sage.

Financial Times (2003) '*Humanity on the move: the myths and realities of international migration*', 30 July.

Georgiou, M. (2001) 'Crossing the boundaries of the ethnic home. Media consumption and ethnic identity construction in the public space: the case of the Cypriot Community Centre in North London', *Gazette*, 63 (4): 311–30.

Giddens, A. (1990) *The Consequences of Modernity*. Cambridge: Polity.

Giddens, A. (1991) *Modernity and Self-Identity: Self and Society in the Late Modern Age*. Cambridge: Polity.

Gillespie, M. (1995) *Television, Ethnicity and Cultural Change*. London: Routledge.

Golding, P. and Harris, P. (1997) *Beyond Cultural Imperialism: Globalization, Communication and the New International Order*. London: Sage.

Hall, S. (1991) 'The local and the global: globalization and ethnicities', pp. 19–40 in A.D. Kind (ed.) *Culture, Globalization and the World System*. London: Macmillan.

Hall, S. (1996) 'Who needs identity?', pp. 1–17 in S. Hall and P. du Gay (eds) *Questions of Cultural Identity*. London: Sage.

Hamelink, C.J. (1983) *Cultural Autonomy in Global Communications*. New York: Longman.

Hannerz, U. (1990) 'Cosmopolitans and locals in world culture', pp. 237–52 in M. Featherstone (ed.) *Global Culture: Nationalism, Globalization and Modernity*. London: Sage.

Harvey, D. (1990) *The Condition of Postmodernity: An Enquiry into the Origins of Cultural Change*. Oxford: Blackwell.

Harvey, D. (1993) 'From space to place and back again: reflections on the condition of postmodernity', pp. 3–29 in J. Bird et al. (eds) *Mapping the Futures: Local Culture, Global Change*. London: Routledge.

Held, D., McGrew, A., Goldblatt, D. and Perraton, J. (1999) *Global Transformations: Politics, Economics and Culture*. Cambridge: Polity.

Herman, E. and McChesney, R.W. (1997) *The Global Media: The New Missionaries of Global Capitalism*. London: Cassell.

Hirst, P. and Thompson, G. (1996) *Globalization in Question*. Cambridge: Polity.

Hong, J. (1998) *The Internationalization of Television in China: The Evolution of Ideology, Society and Media since the Reform*. Westport, CT: Praeger.

Huang, Y. (1994) 'Peaceful evolution: the case of television reform in post-Mao China', *Media, Culture & Society*, 16: 217–41.

Hutchings, G. (2000) *Modern China: A Companion to a Rising Power*. London: Penguin.

Innis, H. (1950) *Empire and Communications*. Toronto: University of Toronto Press.

Kaplún, M. (1973) *La communicación de masas en América Latina*. Bogotá: Asociación de Poblaciones Educativas.

Katz, E. (1971) 'Television comes to the people of the book', pp. 249–70 in I.L. Horowitz (ed.) *The Use and Abuse of Social Science*. New Brunswick, N.J.: Transaction.

Kivikuru, U. (1988) 'From import to modelling: Finland – An Example of Old Periphery Dependency', *European Journal of Communication*, 3: 9–34.

Kuhn, T. (1962) *The Structure of Scientific Revolutions*. Chicago: University of Chicago Press.

Laqueur, W. (1972) *A History of Zionism*. Worcester: Trinity.

Larrain, J. (1994) *Ideology and Cultural Identity: Modernity and the Third World Presence*. Cambridge: Polity Press.

Lash, S. and Urry, J. (1987) *The End of Organized Capitalism*. Madison, WI: University of Wisconsin Press.

Lazarsfeld, P., Berelson, B. and Gaudet, H. (1948) *The People's Choice*. New York: Columbia University Press.

Lie, R. (2002) 'Spaces of intercultural communication', paper presented to Virtual Forum on Intercultural Communication of the 23rd IAMCR Conference, Barcelona, 21–26 July 2002.

Lie, R. and Servaes, J. (2000) 'Globalisation: consumption and identity – towards research nodal points', pp. 307–32 in R. Lie and J. Servaes (eds) *Media and Politics in Transition: Cultural Identity in the Age of Globalization*. London: Routledge.

Liebes, T. and Katz, E. (1990) *The Export of Meaning: Cross-Cultural Readings of 'Dallas'*. Oxford: Oxford University Press.

Lo, S.-H. (2002) 'Diaspora regime into nation: mediating hybrid nationhood in Taiwan', *The Public*, 9 (1): 65–84.

Lopez, G. (2002), *Telecoms and Mobile Communications Services in Israel, 2001–2007*. Middle East and Africa Telecommunications Network Services. An unpublished report.

Lowe, D.M. (1982) *History of Bourgeois Perception*. Chicago: University of Chicago Press.

Lull, J. (1991) *China Turned On: Television, Reform and Resistance*. New York: Routledge.

Lull, J. (2000) *Media, Communication, Culture: A Global Approach*, 2nd edn. Cambridge: Polity.

Mackerras, C., Taneja, P. and Young, G. (1998) *China since 1978*, 2nd edn. Melbourne: Addison Wesley Longman.

Mäenpää, P. (2001) 'Mobile communication as way of urban life', pp. 107–24 in J. Gronow and A. Warde (eds) *Ordinary Consumption*. London: Routledge.

Marcus, G. (1998) *Ethnography through Thick and Thin*. Princeton, NJ: Princeton University Press.

Martin-Barbero, J. (1993) *Communication, Culture and Hegemony: From the Media to Mediations*. London: Sage.

Massey, D. (1994) *Space, Place and Gender*. Cambridge: Polity.

Mattelart, A. (1979) *Multinational Corporations and the Control of Culture*. Brighton: Harvester.

Mattelart, A. (2000) *Networking the World, 1794–2000*. Minneapolis: University of Minnesota Press.

McGuigan, J. (1992) *Cultural Populism*. New York: Routledge.

McLuhan, M. (1964) *Understanding Media: The Extensions of Man*. London: Routledge, 2002.

McLuhan, M. and Fiore, Q. (1967) *The Medium is the Message: An Inventory of Effects*. New York: Bantam.

McQuail, D. (1994) *Mass Communication Theory: An Introduction*. London: Sage.

McQuail, D. and Windahl, S. (1993) *Communication Models for the Study of Mass Communications*. London: Longman.

Merrill, J. and Fischer, H.-D. (1970) *International Communication: Media, Channels, Functions*. New York: Hastings.

Meyrowitz, M. (1985) *No Sense of Place: The Impact of Electronic Media on Social Behaviour*. Oxford: Oxford University Press.

Mohammadi, A. (ed.) (1997) *International Communication and Globalization*. London: Sage.

Morley, D. and Robins, K. (1995) *Spaces of Identity: Global Media, Electronic Landscapes and Cultural Boundaries*. London: Routledge.

Mowlana, H. (1997) *Global Information and World Communication*, 2nd edn. London: Sage.

Mumford, L. (1986) *The Future of Technics and Civilization*. London: Freedom.

Mykänen, J. (2003) 'Kiinalaisten Internet on kotimainen ehdonalaisvanki,' *Helsingin Sanomat*, 18 August.

Ohmae, K. (1995) *The End of the Nation-State: The Rise of Regional Economies*. London: Harper Collins.

Ong, W.J. (1982) *Orality and Literacy: the Technology of the World*. London: Methuen.

Osborn, A. (2001) 'UK at bottom of languages class', *The Guardian*, 20 February.

Pasquali, A. (1963) *Comunicación y cultura de masas*. Caracas: Universidad Central de Venezuela.

Pieterse, J.N. (1995) 'Globalization as hybridization', pp. 45–68 in M. Featherstone, S. Lash and R. Robertson (eds) *Global Modernities*. London: Sage.

Price, M.E. (1995) *Television, the Public Sphere, and National Identity*. Oxford: Clarendon.

Rantanen, T. (2000) 'The future of Nordic media and communication studies: the end of a splendid isolation', *Nordicom Information*, 22 (2): 37–42.

Rantanen, T. (2002) *The Global and the National: Media and Communications in Post-Communist Russia*. Lanham, MD: Rowman & Littlefield.

Rantanen, T. (2003) 'New sense of place in the 19th century news', *Media, Culture & Society*, 24 (4): 435–50.

Relph, E. (1976) *Place and Placelessness*. London: Pion.

Reyes Matta, F. (1977) *La información en el nuevo orden internacional*. Mexico: Instituto Latinoamericano de Etudios Transnacionales.

Rheingold, H. (2002) *Smart Mobs: The Next Social Revolution*. Cambridge: Perseus.

Roach, C. (1997) 'Cultural imperialism and resistance in media theory and literary theory', *Media, Culture & Society*, 19 (1): 47–66.

Robbins, B. and Cheah, P. (eds) (1998) *Cosmopolitics: Thinking and Feeling beyond the Nation*. Minneapolis: University of Minnesota Press.

Robertson, R. (1990) 'Mapping the global condition: globalisation as the central concept', *Theory, Culture & Society*, 7 (2–3): 15–30.

Robertson, R. (1992) *Globalization: Social Theory and Global Culture*. London: Sage.

Robertson, R. (1995) 'Globalization: time–space and homogeneity–heterogeneity', pp. 25–44 in M. Featherstone (ed.) *Global Modernities*. London: Sage.

Rowe, W. and Schelling, V. (1991) *Memory and Modernity: Popular Culture in Latin America*. London: Verso.

Said, E. (1993) *Culture and Imperialism*. London: Routledge.

Saukko, P. (2003) *Doing Research in Cultural Studies: An Introduction to Classical and New Methodological Approaches*. London: Sage.

Scannell, P. (1989) 'Public service broadcasting and modern life', *Media, Culture & Society*, 11 (1): 135–66.

Schiller, H. (1976) *Communications and Cultural Dominations*. New York: Sharpe.

Schlesinger, P. (1987) 'On national identity: some conceptions and misconceptions criticised', *Social Science Information*, 26 (2): 219–64.

Schlesinger, P. (1991) *Media, State and Nation: Political Violence and Collective Identities*. London: Sage.

Short, J.R. and Kim, Y.-H. (1999) *Globalization and the City*. New York: Longman.

Silverstone, R. (1999) *Why Study the Media?* London: Sage.

Sinclair, J., Jacka, E. and Cunningham, S. (1996) *New Patterns in Global Television: Peripheral Vision*. New York: Oxford University Press.

Skapinger, M. (2000) 'The tongue twisters', *Financial Times*, 28 December.

Sklair, L. (2002) *Globalization: Capitalism and its Alternatives*. Oxford: Oxford University Press.

Smith, A. (1990) 'Towards a global culture?', pp. 171–92 in M. Featherstone (ed.) *Global Culture*. London: Sage

Smythe, D.W. (1981) *Dependency Road: Communications, Capitalism, Consciousness and Canada*. Norwood, NJ: Ablex.

Song, J. (2003) 'How media contribute to a peasant's attitude towards globalization in a Chinese village'. Unpublished MSc dissertation. Department of Media and Communication, London School of Economics and Political Science.

Sparks, C. (1998) 'Is there a global public sphere?', pp. 108–24 in D.K. Thussu (ed.) *Electronic Empires: Global Media and Local Resistance*. London: Arnold.

Sreberny, A. (1996) 'The global and the local in international communications', pp. 177–203 in J. Curran and M. Gurevitch (eds) *Mass Media and Society*, 2nd edn. London: Arnold.

Stephens, M. (1989) *A History of News*. New York: Penguin Books.

Straubhaar, T. (1991) 'Beyond media imperialism: asymmetrical interdependence and cultural proximity', *Critical Studies in Mass Communication*, 8 (1): 39–59.

Thompson, J.B. (1995) *The Media and Modernity*. Cambridge: Polity.

Thussu, D.K. (ed.) (1998) *Electronic Empires: Global Media and Local Resistance*. London: Arnold.

Thussu, D.K. (2000) *International Communication: Continuity and Change*. London: Arnold.

Tomlinson, J. (1991) *Cultural Imperialism: A Critical Introduction*. London: Pinter.

Tomlinson, J. (1994) 'A phenomenology of globalisation? Giddens on global modernity', *European Journal of Communication*, 9(2): 149–72.

Tomlinson, J. (1997) 'Cultural globalization and cultural imperialism', pp. 170–90 in A. Mohammadi (ed.) *International Communication and Globalization: A Critical Introduction*. London: Sage.

Tomlinson, J. (1999) *Globalization and Culture*. Cambridge: Polity.

Tönnies, F. (1926) *Gemeinschaft und Gesellschaft, Grundbegriffe der reinen Soziologie*. Berlin: Curtius.

Tunstall, J. (1977) *The Media are American*. London: Constable.

Tunstall, J. and Machin, D. (1999) *The Anglo-American Media Connection*. Oxford: Oxford University Press.

Virtanen, L. and Dubois, T. (2000) *Finnish Folklore*. Helsinki: Finnish Literature Society.

Waters, M. (1995) *Globalisation*. London: Routledge.

Williams, R. (1977) *Marxism and Literature*. Oxford: Oxford University Press.

Williams, R. (1980) *The Long Revolution*. Harmondsworth: Penguin.

Zerubavel, E. (1982) 'The standardization of time: a sociohistorical perspective,' *American Journal of Sociology*, 88 (1): 1–23.

Zerubavel, E. (2003) *Time Maps: Collective Memory and the Social Shape of the Past*. Chicago: University of Chicago Press.

INDEX